Bishop Joseph Blount Cheshire

Photograph by Bayard Wootten
BISHOP JOSEPH BLOUNT CHESHIRE
From a portrait by Mrs. Arthur Nash, in the possession of Miss Sarah Cheshire, Raleigh, North Carolina.

Bishop
JOSEPH BLOUNT CHESHIRE

His Life and Work

BY LAWRENCE FOUSHEE LONDON, Ph.D.
Historiographer of the Diocese of North Carolina

Chapel Hill

THE UNIVERSITY OF NORTH CAROLINA PRESS

1941

COPYRIGHT, 1941,
BY THE UNIVERSITY OF NORTH CAROLINA PRESS

DESIGNED BY STEFAN SALTER

Foreword

By EDWIN A. PENICK, Bishop of North Carolina

One of the many characteristics for which Bishop Cheshire is remembered by his friends and admirers was his uncompromising adherence to the last letter of truth. An inaccurate or careless remark often brought forth from him a startling correction. His own historical papers were loyal to such facts as patient research could discover. His official documents were models of lucidity and precision. His counsel was penetrating and true and bracing like fresh air in a stuffy room. His conversation, particularly when he was describing the very human traits of men and women he had known, was full of delightful surprises because of his breathtaking forthrightness. He even carried in his pocketbook an exact paper pattern of a hugh mountain trout he once caught as documentary evidence of his best fish story.

This characteristic of Bishop Cheshire must have been in the author's mind when he wrote the following pages. I believe that the good Bishop would approve this biography for its restraint and disciplined faithfulness to the record of a true life.

Ravenscroft
Raleigh, North Carolina
February 10, 1941.

Preface

From my earliest memories I can recall the annual visits of Bishop Cheshire to the home of my parents. As very young boys my brothers and I were fond of looking at him, for with his flowing white beard and rather stocky figure, he appeared a perfect embodiment of Santa Claus. He readily gained our confidence with his frank and open manner and his keen understanding of the sort of things children were interested in. As I grew older he won my complete affection and admiration. With his many relatives and friends throughout North Carolina, I felt particularly honored when he wrote me letters from England during his visit there in 1920. The multiplicity of such personal attentions was one of his characteristics which gained for him the lasting affection of his people.

Although I have felt inadequate to the task of writing Bishop Cheshire's life, I have found the work a labor of love and a distinct privilege. Some persons will undoubtedly be disappointed that more stories of and about the Bishop have not been included. The use of many of his anecdotes has purposefully been avoided, since most of them are much more delightfully told by the Bishop himself in his charming volume of reminiscences, *Nonnulla*. My primary object has been to present his accomplishments as deacon, priest, and bishop. His work in these periods of his career merits preservation in some permanent form for its own sake as well as for the benefit of future churchmen. Also, an attempt has been made to portray the Bishop's dynamic personality and its striking influence upon the character of his work and of his human contacts.

I wish to gratefully acknowledge the kind assistance given me by Mr. Joseph B. Cheshire, Miss Sarah Cheshire, and Mr. James W. Cheshire in reading this work and for the generous loan of invaluable manuscripts. I also wish to express my appreciation to my wife, Emily Dewey, for her untiring help in criticizing and reworking the manuscript, and to Bishop Edwin Anderson Penick and Rev. Alfred S. Lawrence for reading the work.

Lawrence F. London

Chapel Hill, North Carolina
December 1, 1940.

Contents

		PAGE
	FOREWORD, BY BISHOP EDWIN A. PENICK	v
	PREFACE	vii
CHAPTER		
I	YOUTH AND MANHOOD	1
II	DEACON AND PRIEST	18
III	SAINT PETER'S PARISH	27
IV	ELECTION TO THE EPISCOPATE	46
V	FIRST YEARS IN THE EPISCOPACY	55
VI	MAN AND BISHOP	77
VII	HISTORIAN	88
VIII	WORK AMONG THE COLORED PEOPLE	99
IX	DEVELOPMENT AND CONCLUSION OF THE BISHOP'S WORK	109
	NOTES	127
	PUBLISHED WRITINGS OF JOSEPH BLOUNT CHESHIRE	131
	INDEX	135

Bishop Joseph Blount Cheshire

CHAPTER I

Youth and Manhood

It was eleven o'clock one morning in the middle of September, 1869, when Joseph Blount Cheshire stepped into a classroom to teach a course in Latin. Before him sat six boys, several of them older than himself. He was only nineteen years old, and he was about to begin his first job. The school was St. Clement's Hall at Ellicott City, Maryland, and the assignment for that day was one in Sallust. About all young Cheshire could recall of that particular passage was its being one of the most difficult he had ever tried to translate. He was faced with the alternative of bluffing his way through or frankly confessing to the boys that he was thoroughly unprepared to teach the assignment. So, boldly facing his class, he declared: "Young gentlemen, it is many years since I last looked into Sallust, and this passage, Caesar's speech, I remember as the most difficult passage in this book. I am not prepared to deal with it today, but I will endeavor to be ready for you tomorrow."

This was a rule of life which he followed consistently, to deal frankly and honestly with every situation, no matter what it might cost him personally. Complete fearlessness was one of Bishop Cheshire's most pronounced characteristics. In his announced views on public questions, in the administration of his diocese, and in his historical writings, his courage was often manifested. His was not, however, a character which could be described in a few striking phrases. The man can best be understood by observing his deeds as they developed from early youth until the end of a long life of four score and two years.

In the mid-nineteenth century the quiet little town of Tarboro, North Carolina, was like many other small towns to be found in the Old South. It was one of the oldest places in the state, having been founded in the colonial period and given the distinction of a borough town. Tarboro contained a fairly large number of old established families and a few persons of some prominence in the state. Not the least of these was the Rev. Joseph Blount Cheshire, Rector of Calvary Episcopal Church, a man who exemplified in his life and work the best traditions of the Episcopal clergy.

Dr. Cheshire came of an old North Carolina family which for several generations had lived in the Albemarle section. One of his ancestors was Joseph Blount, who was a member of the first vestry of St. Paul's parish, Edenton. His parents, John Cheshire and Elizabeth Blount, lived in Edenton, where he was born in December, 1814. He received his education at the Edenton Academy and at the Episcopal School for Boys. The latter school had just been founded by Bishop Ives and was located in Raleigh on the site where now stands St. Mary's Junior College. After completing his course at the Episcopal School, he took up the study of law in Raleigh under the supervision of Thomas P. Devereux.

Youth and Manhood

In 1836 he was admitted to the bar, but he evidently did not find the law congenial to his tastes, for he soon abandoned it. He decided to enter the ministry, and in 1838 began his studies for that field of work under the direction of Bishop Ives. During his preparation for the ministry he made the acquaintance of the botanist and clergyman, Dr. M. Ashley Curtis. The interest which Dr. Curtis stimulated in him for plants and flowers bore abundant fruit. The beautiful grounds surrounding Calvary Church stand today as a living expression of his love for flowers and shrubs.

By February, 1840, Dr. Cheshire had advanced sufficiently far in his theological studies to be ordained deacon by Bishop Ives. The Bishop placed him in charge of the parishes at Halifax and Windsor. The next year he was ordained priest and was given Calvary Church, Tarboro, in addition to his other work. Shortly after taking over this work he organized a mission at Scotland Neck, which in time became Trinity parish. Three parishes and a mission was a large assignment for a young clergyman, but Dr. Cheshire was not daunted by the extent of his duties. From the first his chief interest was in the work at Tarboro. In consequence of this and the desire of the Calvary Church people for more of his time, he gave up the church at Halifax in 1848 and the one at Windsor the following year. He retained his work at Scotland Neck, however, until 1869. His pastorate at Calvary Church continued for more than half a century. During this long rectorship a beautiful new church was built, to which he himself contributed generously.

Dr. Cheshire will probably be best remembered in the history of the American Episcopal Church for the part he played in healing the breach between the northern and southern branches of the church following the close of the Civil War. He waged a determined fight in the diocesan convention of 1865 to send deputies to the General Convention to be held that fall in Philadelphia. The advocates of reconciliation were successful, and Dr. Cheshire was elected one of the deputies to the General Convention. At Philadelphia he used all his influence in helping to bring about the reunion of the church.

Two years after he took charge of Calvary parish, Dr. Cheshire was married to Elizabeth Toole Parker, daughter of Theophilus Parker, his senior warden, and Mary Toole Parker. The next most important event in his life was the birth of his son and namesake, Joseph Blount, who was born on March 27, 1850. In the course of time Dr. and Mrs. Cheshire had five other children, Theophilus Parker, John, Elizabeth, Annie Gray, and Katherine Drane. John and Elizabeth, however, died in their second year.

Joseph Blount was born in the house built many years before by his grandfather, Theophilus Parker. His father and mother had lived in it since their marriage and had come into its possession after the death of his grandfather. When Joseph was born his parents' household consisted of themselves, his grandmother, an aunt, and two cousins. With the subsequent births of his brothers and sisters his family was indeed a large one. The give and take of a large family probably played some part in the development of the tolerant and unselfish character which so distinguished him in manhood.

Young Cheshire received his earliest education under the direction of his mother, who taught him reading, writing, and something about numbers. He did not at-

Youth and Manhood 5

tend a formal school until he was nine years old. However, he found himself to be "quite as far advanced in the knowledge of books as the most forward" of his companions. The school he first attended in Tarboro was taught by Rev. and Mrs. Owen. It was while attending this school that he and Richard Lewis met one another and formed a friendship which grew and continued for more than three-score years.

In the fall of 1861 Cheshire entered the Tarboro Male Academy, whose sole teacher at that time was Mr. Frank S. Wilkinson, a graduate of the University of North Carolina. In this school Wilkinson took boys of every age, from beginners to those preparing for college. Cheshire later tells us that Wilkinson was devoted to the profession of teaching, laboring "faithfully to interest his pupils, and give them the best that he had himself." The school usually numbered between thirty and thirty-five boys, but when it included as many as forty, Wilkinson engaged an assistant. During Cheshire's attendance at the Academy, Mr. William Henry Johnston was employed as an assistant. He was also a graduate of the University and, as Cheshire says, "a very good scholar after the standards of the day." In this small school, which never boasted more than two teachers at any one time, Joseph Cheshire prepared himself for college.

Since the summer climate of Tarboro did not agree with Dr. Cheshire's health, he purchased in 1850 a home in Franklin County, about four miles from Louisburg. This place was named Monreath and on it stood an old, well-built house surrounded by one hundred and sixty acres of land. Here the Cheshires spent their summers. These pleasant vacations at Monreath caused Joseph to lose about two months of school each year, since the fall term began the middle of July. Therefore, in the summer of 1864 he asked his father if he could not attend the Louisburg Academy from July to September. His father readily agreed, and each day young Cheshire walked the four miles into Louisburg to conjugate Latin verbs and pursue the other fields of learning which made up the curriculum of the average classical school of that day.

During the Civil War the Cheshires did not suffer from molestation by the enemy or from severe deprivation as did many southern families. They gave shelter and comfort to many refugees from the eastern part of the state, which was occupied by federal troops. Writing of his impressions of the war years, Cheshire observed: "It is strange that almost all my memories of those tragical days seem to be of bright and happy experiences. I do not remember any atmosphere of gloom or depression. The spirit of all was brave and bouyant."[1] The abolition of slavery did not greatly affect the economic status of his family, since his father owned only a few domestic servants whom he had inherited.

Cheshire's religious education began, of course, at home. Every Sunday afternoon he and his brother stood before their mother with the Negro children and repeated their assigned part of the catechism. He did not attend Sunday school until after he had learned all the catechism, that is, all but the "Desire." He later remarked that he never learned it "so as not to forget it," and that it was the only thing he ever tried to remember and failed.

By the fall of 1865 Cheshire was ready to enter college. It had been originally planned that he should go to the University of North Carolina. But when the time arrived his father did not have the money to send him. Dr. Cheshire, however, had already decided not to send his son to the state University; he did not think the environment there would be suitable for a boy of fifteen, for a good many young soldiers, fresh from the careless life of the army, were entering the University that fall. Cheshire's best friend, Dick Lewis, and several others of his class-mates went in the fall of 1865 to Mr. Graves' school in Granville County. He was left in a class by himself at the Tarboro Academy, where he continued his studies under the direction of Mr. Wilkinson.

During this period of study at the Academy Cheshire wrote an amusing and original essay on the subject of honesty. Launching into his subject with the statement that there had already been so much written upon it that it was about worn out, he declared that he chose the topic for want of a better one. This introduction was succeeded by the following:

> "I have been thinking for a long time what else to say about 'Honesty,' but can't think of a single thing which some other boy has not said in his composition since I have been going to school: and I think that I had better practice what I have here attempted to preach, and tell you, Mr. Wilkinson, that it is Monday morning, and that composition never entered into my head Saturday, and so you need not expect much. Instead of a composition I will give you an account of my doings Saturday evening, which I hope you will take as an equivalent."

Cheshire then gave an interesting description of a delightful horseback ride he had had with a young lady. He concluded his essay by saying: "I hope this will be taken as a composition. If it is not I hope you will return it as there is enough clean paper on it to write another one." [2] The composition is not only worth quoting for its originality, but also because it brings out a pronounced characteristic of the later man. Complete honesty with himself as well as others, under all conditions, was one of his most outstanding qualities.

Joseph continued his studies under Mr. Wilkinson until February, 1866. By that time Dr. Cheshire had secured sufficient funds with which to send his son to college. He was still opposed to sending him to the University for the reason already mentioned and because he felt the fate of that institution at the time was most uncertain. He decided, therefore, to send Joseph to Trinity College at Hartford, Connecticut. Trinity was an excellent school, under the management of the church, and Dr. Cheshire was personally acquainted with its president.

Before his son left home for college, Dr. Cheshire told him that he must decide while in school what he wished to do for his life's work. He explained that since he had other children to educate, he would not be able to help him after graduation. His father went on to say that it would be a great happiness to him if his son should decide to go into the ministry, but that was something he must determine for himself. Cheshire later remarked that this was the only time in his memory that his father ever spoke to him of the possibility of making the ministry his life's work.

In late February of 1866 young Cheshire left home for Hartford. An inexperienced boy, having traveled little beyond his section of the state, he now set out to enter a strange school among people with whom, less than a year ago, his people had been at war. Such a

Youth and Manhood 9

prospect would have filled an older heart with trepidation. He traveled as far as New York with a stranger who had been in Tarboro on business, and from thence he went alone to Hartford.

Cheshire was allowed to enter the Freshman class with conditions only in Greek and Latin composition, which was a tribute to the work done under Mr. Wilkinson that fall. He learned upon arriving at school that he was the first man from the Confederate States to enter Trinity since the close of the war. He was treated kindly by his fellow students, and never complained of any hostility or unfriendliness on the part of the northern boys. His closest friends, however, were among a group of students from Maryland.

Shortly after he entered college, his father wrote to President Kerfoot asking him to suggest someone on the faculty who would be willing to act as an advisor and friend to his son. Dr. Kerfoot proposed Rev. William W. Niles, Professor of Latin at Trinity, who gladly took Cheshire under his care. In time the two became fast friends. Professor Niles and his wife often entertained him and always made him feel at home in their house. Under Professor Niles' direction Cheshire was prepared for confirmation, and in May, 1866, he was confirmed in the college chapel. In later years he said of the Nileses: "I can never be sufficiently grateful to Professor Niles and his good wife. . . . I enjoyed from that time—from my Freshman days in college to the end of their lives, the friendship and confidence of these most admirable people." [3]

Dr. Cheshire had a good deal of difficulty in maintaining his son at college. The years immediately following the war were hard ones for almost all southerners, and the Cheshire family was no exception. When Cheshire came home for the Christmas holidays of 1867, his father told him that he would be unable to send him back to college. He accepted this decision as final, and wrote his roommate, Robert F. Bixby, that he was not returning to college after the holidays. Not long afterwards, Dr. Cheshire received a letter from Professor Pynchon, a member of the Trinity faculty, who informed him that a friend, who wished to withhold his name, would be happy to advance the necessary money for his son's monthly board if that would be sufficient to make his return to college possible. After talking the matter over with his son, Dr. Cheshire accepted the generous offer, since he believed he would be able to repay the full amount by the end of 1868. In this way young Cheshire was able to resume his work at Trinity, receiving each month through Dr. Pynchon the money for his board. As he had anticipated, Dr. Cheshire was able to repay the whole debt at the end of 1868. Although he never knew, Cheshire suspected that the money, so badly needed at the time, came from the father of his friend, Robert Bixby.

During his first two years at Trinity, Cheshire had come to know Rev. John Williams, Bishop of Connecticut and one-time Presiding Bishop of the Episcopal Church, who often visited the college. When school closed in June, 1868, Cheshire found that he was not financially able to go home for the summer vacation, and that he would have to remain in Hartford. Bishop Williams heard of his plans and thereupon invited him to his old home in Deerfield, Massachusetts, for a month. The Bishop said that he could serve as his secretary, and on this condition Cheshire gladly accepted the invitation.

Youth and Manhood

As it turned out, he had very little to do. He spent the month most delightfully, meeting many interesting people and visiting near-by historical places. After leaving Bishop Williams, he spent a pleasant month in Maryland visiting two of his college friends. Thus most of the summer passed rapidly, and he returned to Hartford greatly refreshed, ready to begin the last year of his collegiate work.

While at Trinity Cheshire became a member of the Phi Kappa fraternity, now the Alpha Delta Phi. He was the only member of his class who belonged to this fraternity. Consequently, Cheshire modestly explains, whenever an honor fell to a Phi Kappa of his class he was the only one to receive it. Whether this was the reason or not, he was made president of the Senior class, and was elected a marshal for the commencement of 1868. As for class and college prizes, he never entered a contest until his last year. At this time he entered the competition for the "Tuttle Prize," which was an award of thirty dollars for the best essay by a senior on a subject to be chosen by the faculty. The topic selected for Cheshire's class was "The Causes of the French Revolution." Cheshire submitted a paper of forty-eight foolscap pages. Much to his gratification, and somewhat to his surprise, his essay won the prize. With the money he purchased "Pratt's Complete Works of Bishop Hall" in ten volumes as a gift for his father. For himself he bought a set of Chaucer's works in eight volumes and a few other books. Indeed, he seems to have made his prize money go far and to much advantage.

In June, 1869, Cheshire's college days came to a close. During his three and one-half years at Trinity he made many close friendships which continued throughout his life. He was not an outstanding student, but did creditably in all his courses. At the commencement exercises he delivered an original address, which was required of all graduates. He chose as the subject of his senior oration "The Strength of Republican Governments," a topic characteristic of that period. Cheshire had been influenced in the choice of this subject by De Tocqueville's *Democracy in America*, in which he had become interested. Following his graduation he returned to North Carolina, where he spent the summer of 1869 with his family at Monreath. This was his last long vacation. He was soon to take over his first position and to begin earning for the remainder of his life his own way.

In the course of graduation week at Trinity, Cheshire had the good fortune of making the acquaintance of Rev. John Avery Shepherd of Maryland. Dr. Shepherd had organized a few years before a private school, which he called St. Clement's Hall, at Ellicott City near Baltimore. Being favorably impressed with Cheshire's personality and his record at Trinity, Dr. Shepherd offered him a position in his school teaching Latin and Greek for the scholastic year 1869–70. His salary was to be six hundred dollars a year in addition to board and lodging. Cheshire gladly accepted the position, since he wished no longer to be a burden on his father. His younger brother was then ready to enter college and was only waiting for him to finish.

In the middle of September Cheshire left Monreath to take up his duties at St. Clement's Hall. Before he left home his father gave him fifty dollars to aid him until he should receive a part of his salary. This was the last time he ever gave him any money, that is, from a feeling of responsibility for his son's support.

Youth and Manhood 13

At St. Clement's Cheshire was given all the upper classes in Latin and Greek, and in addition taught some arithmetic and algebra. In consequence of his rather poor beginning in Latin and Greek at the Tarboro Academy, he never became a scholar in these fields. While teaching Latin he became more interested in this subject and read rather widely in Tacitus and other Latin authors. In the course of his busy life of teaching he found time to continue "a kind of study" of Blackstone which he had begun in his senior year at Trinity. He also read through Kent's *Commentaries* and a good deal of English poetry.

Cheshire came to know a number of people in the neighborhood of the school who helped to make his life at St. Clement's more interesting and pleasant. He spent a good many week-ends in Baltimore with some of his Trinity friends. When his oldest and best friend, Richard Lewis, came to Baltimore to study medicine in the fall of 1870, his visits became more frequent. On the whole, his life at St. Clement's was happy, and the experience he gained, worth while. He never, however, became fond of teaching, but he enjoyed his students and took a warm personal interest in them. After two years at St. Clement's he decided to abandon teaching for the law profession, which he thought would be more congenial to his tastes.

When Cheshire returned to North Carolina in June, 1871, he went with his family to Hillsboro to spend the summer. Here he began the study of law under the eminent lawyer, William K. Ruffin, son of Chief Justice Thomas Ruffin, who coached law students since he was too crippled to do much active practice. Ruffin was a "devotee" of the common law and always gave his students a thorough drilling in it. He made Cheshire devote almost all the summer to the study of Second Blackstone and Cruise's *Real Property*. When he left Hillsboro in September, Ruffin made him promise that he would secure an old folio edition of Coke's *Commentaries on Littleton* and read it carefully. Some time later Cheshire bought a copy of this work in Baltimore and read it from cover to cover as he had promised. He once remarked that he believed he was the last man in North Carolina to have completely read the old folio edition. Cheshire found Mr. William Ruffin "a most interesting man as well as a stimulating and helpful teacher." [4]

Upon returning to Tarboro Cheshire continued his study of law, now in the office of Howard and Perry. In this office he "read law," for he says that Judge George Howard would not agree to give him any instruction. Cheshire, however, maintained that he learned much law from Judge Howard, and "a good deal of sound practical wisdom."

After his summer's work under William Ruffin and some three months' study in Judge Howard's office, Cheshire was ready to try for his license. On January 1, 1872, he went to Raleigh to be examined by the Supreme Court Justices. It was an oral test and, in Cheshire's own words, was "a very slight and superficial examination" in comparison with those given today. The day after the examination he was informed that he had passed and was granted his license.

Shortly afterwards George G. Hooper, a Trinity College friend, wrote Cheshire to come to Baltimore and join him in a law partnership. He did not particularly care to leave North Carolina, but he feared if he remained he might be a burden on his father while establishing himself. He accordingly accepted Hooper's offer, and the two men formed a partnership under the firm name of Hooper and Cheshire. Hooper agreed to pay him a salary for the first year, at the end of which time they would make a new agreement.

Cheshire had not been in the office long before he learned that Hooper had "little real law practice." His work was almost entirely confined to drawing up conveyances and examining land titles. After some fifteen months of this sort of work, Cheshire realized there was little future for him in such a partnership. It was, therefore, with much pleasure that he received, in May, 1873, a letter from his friend, John L. Bridgers, Jr., asking him to return to Tarboro and join him and his father, Colonel John L. Bridgers, in the practice of law. Cheshire readily accepted this proposal, and the following month came back to North Carolina where he was to make his home for the remainder of his life.

Cheshire was happy to be living in Tarboro once again with his family and among his old friends. Thus was formed the firm of Bridgers, Cheshire, and Bridgers. This connection continued until January, 1875, at which time Cheshire was offered the position of secretary and treasurer of the Pamlico Banking and Insurance Company, a corporation organized to solicit fire insurance. He accepted the offer because it gave him an office and a small salary and did not interfere with his law practice. The company's business was not extensive, and required only a few hours of his time each day. While holding this position he was also treasurer of the Tarboro Building and Loan Association. Again this office demanded little of his time, merely requiring that he receive the money from the secretary weekly and pay it out upon his order.

Cheshire continued the practice of law until the early part of 1878. In summing up his work at the bar, he observed: "I made a living and saved a few hundred dollars. I had no very interesting or important cases, so far as I recall." [5] During his last year of practice, however, he made a little over fifteen hundred dollars, which, for a young lawyer of that period, was doing quite well.

Since leaving St. Clement's Hall in June, 1871, Cheshire had not by any means devoted all of his time and thought to the study and practice of law. He accomplished a great deal more in the summer of 1871 than the study of common law under Mr. William K. Ruffin. It was then that he renewed his acquaintance with his cousin, Miss Annie Huske Webb, who lived in Hillsboro. He had seen this cousin but little since her visit to Tarboro in December, 1865. He always remembered the first time he saw her upon her arrival in Tarboro for that visit and described the meeting thus: "When I looked at her, as she came in out of the rain, and lifted the veil from her face, I thought her the most beautiful person I had ever seen. I think that first impression was never effaced." [6]

In the course of the summer spent in Hillsboro Cheshire saw a good deal of his cousin. It was not long before he realized that he was in love with her. While not possessing a particularly romantic nature, Cheshire was a man of deep emotions and fine sentiments. During his courtship of Miss Webb he composed for her this little poem:

Youth and Manhood
A. H. W.

My Love is a fair white Lily,
    And she loves not the day's full glare,
But she seeks out a quiet valley,
    And she lifts up her sweet face there.
The blue heavens through the branches
    Look down with their kindly light;
And she smiles back a gentle greeting
    When the stars look through at night.
The song-birds sing to her sweetly,
    And she's rocked by the gentle breeze;
And she hides from the storms of Winter
    'Midst the roots of the giant trees.
She peeps in the crystal streamlet,
    As she nods in the breezes light:
And she knows not her own fair beauty,
    But is glad that she's pure and white.[7]

By May, 1872, Cheshire and Annie Huske Webb were engaged; but it was not until 1874 that he felt he was financially able to marry. On December 17 of that year they were married in St. Matthew's Church, Hillsboro. They had a simple wedding with Richard Lewis as his best man. The following day Cheshire and his wife went to Tarboro, where for the next four years they made their home with his family.

With this, the greatest event in his life up to that time, we close the first phase of Cheshire's career. During the period he had grown to manhood, received his scholastic and collegiate education, taught for two years, studied law and practiced it for six years, and had some little part in the business world. All of this training and varied experience gave him a rich background for the great work which lay ahead of him.

CHAPTER II

Deacon and Priest

Ever since he left college Cheshire had been conscious of a growing desire to become a candidate for Holy Orders. Not long after his marriage he spoke to his wife of this aspiration, and told her he had now decided to present himself to the Bishop. He had not come to this decision earlier because he was determined not to go into the ministry until he had made a success of what he was doing at that time. He would not enter the ministry as a failure from another field of work. By the middle of 1876 he decided that he was making a respectable living for his wife and himself. He thereupon told his father of his decision and sent Bishop Atkinson his application. Shortly afterwards the Bishop accepted him as a candidate for Holy Orders, and Cheshire began preparing himself for his new work.

It was Cheshire's original plan to attend the General Theological Seminary in New York for a year or two, but Bishop Atkinson and his father dissuaded him from this course because they objected to the Dean of the Seminary and because they felt that its ritualistic influences were too strong. Bishop Atkinson thought that,

Deacon and Priest

since Cheshire had had a good classical education, had pursued intellectual interests, and had been reared in a clergyman's family, he could quite adequately do his preparatory work at home. Cheshire accepted the Bishop's advice, and at once began a well laid-out course of reading. He had already read a good many ecclesiastical works, since he had been contemplating this step for some time.

At the end of 1877 he gave up his connection with the Pamlico Insurance and Banking Company, and soon afterwards concluded his legal affairs. In September, 1877, he went to Raleigh to stand his examinations for the diaconate before Rev. Dr. Matthias M. Marshall and Rev. John E. C. Smedes. Having passed his examinations acceptably, Cheshire was ordained deacon by Bishop Atkinson on April 21, 1878, in Calvary Church, Tarboro. His father presented him for ordination. The following Sunday he assisted his father in the morning service and preached his first sermon. Thus he was launched upon a new career in which he was to rise to heights far beyond his modest dreams.

When Dr. Kemp Plummer Battle, President of the University of North Carolina, heard that Cheshire was studying for the ministry, he asked Bishop Atkinson to send him to Chapel Hill. Dr. Battle was a native of Edgecombe County and had known Cheshire and his family for many years. Since the revival of the University in 1875, Rev. Robert B. Sutton, of Pittsboro, had from time to time held services in the Chapel of the Cross. The Chapel Hill churchmen, however, felt that the parish needed a regular and resident minister. The Bishop complied with Dr. Battle's request and informed Cheshire that he was to serve his diaconate in Chapel Hill under the direction of Dr. Sutton. This was a disappointment to Cheshire, for he had hoped he would be able to remain in Edgecombe County and strengthen the church's position there. The Bishop also directed him to hold a regular appointment in the rapidly growing town of Durham, where as yet there was not even an established mission. This was a difficult assignment for a young deacon just beginning his ministry. In Chapel Hill he had to revive an old parish which had fallen somewhat into decay during the hard years of the reconstruction period, while in Durham he had to build from the ground up, commencing with only a handful of church people.

Cheshire came to Chapel Hill in May, and on the nineteenth of that month held his first service in the Chapel of the Cross. President Battle invited him to make his home at his house until he could find a suitable place. Cheshire accepted this generous offer and spent several weeks with the Battles. In consequence of a long illness, contracted soon after his arrival, he did not hold another service in Chapel Hill until the last Sunday in June. The next Sunday he was able to keep his first appointment in Durham, but following this service, he had a serious relapse and was unable to continue his work until early fall.

For a few weeks that fall Cheshire boarded at the hotel, while his wife visited her family in Hillsboro. This gave him an excellent opportunity to come into close contact with the students, many of whom took their meals at the hotel. In this way he came to know a number of students who were not members of his church. Throughout his rectorship in Chapel Hill he made it a point to know all the students who were in any way connected with the Episcopal Church. In a comparatively short time he was on friendly terms with most of the small student body.

Cheshire frankly confessed that in the first exercise of his ministerial duties among the students he felt "great embarrassment" and even some "timidity." He explained: "I had not been accustomed to speak much of my own religious feelings; and I was at a loss how to make a proper approach to the subject of another person's religious duties and convictions."[1] He visited the boys in their rooms when he thought they liked it, but never sought to force himself upon them. Cheshire later declared he did not remember ever approaching a student on the subject of religion without receiving a serious and courteous hearing. Many students seemed to appreciate the interest he took in their religious life. Cheshire himself was only a few years older than many of the undergraduates and, therefore, could understand their point of view and enter sympathetically into their problems. The effectiveness of his first year's work in Chapel Hill was demonstrated when Bishop Lyman made his visitation to the Chapel of the Cross in May, 1879. Cheshire presented to the Bishop for confirmation nine students and two girls of the village. In later years he remarked that this was "one of the most interesting and satisfactory classes I ever presented."

When he first began preaching, Cheshire took great pains in the preparation of his sermons, writing them out in full. He freely admitted he had "no special gifts or talents as a speaker." In discussing the problem of preaching with Cheshire just after his ordination, Bishop Atkinson said he would give him the same advice which Bishop Johns, of Virginia, used to give his young deacons: "Choose a pretty long text, so that if they persecute you in one city, you may flee to another." Cheshire began, in time, to memorize his sermons and then to attempt to preach extemporaneously, but he always felt that his written sermons were better. Concerning the reception of his sermons in Chapel Hill, he stated: "My Chapel Hill congregation seemed to me most considerate and appreciative of my attempts at preaching, even the students of the University, so far as I could judge." [2]

In his congregation Cheshire had some of the most distinguished members of the University faculty. President Battle was his senior warden and sincere friend, who gave him "judicious praise" as well as sound advice as to the pitfalls which a young clergyman might expect to encounter. Dr. J. de Berniere Hooper, Professor of Greek, was in Cheshire's opinion, "the most scholarly and highly cultivated" member of his parish. Professors Ralph Graves and George T. Winston, both young men who were later to win fame, were also members of his congregation. He lived on friendly relations with these and other members of the small faculty.

When Mrs. Cheshire came to Chapel Hill, she and her husband moved to the home of Dr. William P. Mallett, where they lived until the early part of 1879. They then took over the parish rectory, a small four-room house with a kitchen in the back yard. It faced Rosemary Lane and was situated on a two-acre lot, on part of which stands the present rectory. Their families and parishioners furnished the house for them quite comfortably. There was a small debt on the rectory, and, prior to Cheshire's coming to the parish, it had been rented to assist in retiring the obligation. When he moved into the rectory, he agreed to pay the interest on the debt, notwithstanding that his salary was only five hundred dollars a year. It was not easy, even in those days, to live on such a small income, but Cheshire often remarked that his years in Chapel Hill were "as happy, I believe, as possible in this world." He was fortunate in realizing his happiness at the time and often spoke of it to his wife. To make their happiness complete, a second child,* Elizabeth Toole, was born to them in the summer of 1879.

Although the parish in Chapel Hill was his chief charge, Cheshire did not think that it had an exclusive claim upon him. He regarded it as a center from which to work. In the fall of 1878 he began to lay definite plans for what was to be an important missionary work in Durham. After surveying the prospects there Cheshire, with the co-operation of his little flock, was able to rent a hall on Main Street which was ordinarily used for public entertainments. Here he held services on the first Sunday in every month. The work in Durham prospered remarkably, considering that the congregation had no church building of their own. Cheshire and his congregation soon realized, however, that if much progress was to be made, they must have a church. The greatest difficulty at first was to find a lot within their means. Finally, one was purchased at a low price because of its undesirability from a business standpoint. In the spring of 1880 the foundations of the little church were laid.

Since his congregation could bear only a small part of the cost of building a church, Cheshire had to ask for assistance elsewhere. His family and friends in Edgecombe County contributed about one-fourth of the total cost. In a communication to the *Church Messenger*

* The first child was born in March, 1878, but died only a few days after birth.

Cheshire requested the rectors of the larger parishes of the Diocese to contribute one Sunday's offering to the completion of the Durham church. On the general subject of soliciting aid for religious purposes, he declared: "Indiscriminate begging from anybody and everybody to the neglect of every consideration, except the chance of getting a dollar, is not becoming to the cause of religion, and is a positive discouragement to Christian liberality." This was the kind of soliciting which he never practiced. Throughout his ministry he requested aid for the church of only those who he felt were rightfully responsible for its support.

By the spring of 1881 the church was completed at a cost of about twenty-five hundred dollars. In a remarkably short time, less than a year and a half, the money had been raised and the building erected. Cheshire named it "St. Philip, the Deacon," feeling it to be the "fruit" of his work as a deacon. It was with much pride and happiness that, on July 24, 1881, he assisted Bishop Lyman in the consecration of St. Philip's—a fitting close to his work in that mission.[3]

Cheshire never expected, nor did he ever receive, any compensation from the Diocese for his missionary activities. Concerning extra parochial work, he said: "I did not look upon work outside the parish as extra work, for which I should receive extra remuneration or special commendation."[4] Shortly after Cheshire began his work in Durham, the Treasurer of the Diocese sent him a check for twenty dollars, which he promptly returned, saying that he "did not desire to receive anything from the Diocesan Treasury."[5] During his three years of service in Durham the little mission paid him small amounts from time to time, which approximately covered

Deacon and Priest 25

the expenses he incurred. He looked upon his labors for this mission as "a pure work of love and missionary enterprise." In recalling this experience, he declared: "I believe I worked harder and with more enthusiasm in my Mission of St. Philip's, Durham, and afterwards in establishing St. Mark's Church, Mecklenburg County, than in any other work I ever undertook. . . ." [6]

While carrying forward his constructive work in Chapel Hill and in Durham, Cheshire did not overlook his preparation for the priesthood, although, as he remarked, he did not "feel that impatience to get out of the Diaconate," which he often observed in young clergymen. During his leisure hours he read widely and thoroughly, and was well prepared when the time came for his advancement. At the close of the diocesan convention, held in Winston-Salem, he was ordained priest by Bishop Lyman in St. Paul's Church on May 30, 1880. He was presented for ordination by Rev. John E. C. Smedes, and the sermon for the occasion was preached by Dr. Alfred Watson, later Bishop of East Carolina. Commenting upon the ordination service, the *Church Messenger* said of Cheshire: "thoroughly active, he will do a work that will tell in the diocese."

During his ministry in Chapel Hill Cheshire received calls from several parishes, all of which offered him a better salary than he was then receiving, but he usually declined them by return mail. In the winter of 1881 the vestry of St. Matthew's, Hillsboro, and the church in Burlington asked him to take charge of their parishes. This prospect appealed to him strongly, since he would live in Hillsboro, his wife's old home, where they had many kinsfolk and friends. Before taking any action, however, he consulted Bishop Lyman, who replied that he preferred Cheshire to remain in Chapel Hill where he was doing a good work. He accepted the Bishop's decision and declined the call to Hillsboro.

About two months later Cheshire received a call from St. Peter's, Charlotte, which he declined immediately. Hearing of this action, Bishop Lyman wrote him that he wished him to accept the charge of St. Peter's. Cheshire replied that he had refused to go to Charlotte because the Bishop had instructed him, only a few months earlier, to remain in Chapel Hill. Bishop Lyman, however, answered that he had directed the vestry of St. Peter's to call him again *"and he would see to it"* that Cheshire accepted. The call was accordingly renewed, and Cheshire went to Charlotte to interview the vestry. He told them that he accepted the charge because he felt it his "duty to respect the wishes of the Bishop." Cheshire often remarked that during his ministry he never accepted a call to any parish, explaining that the Bishop had directed him to go to Chapel Hill and later to the parish in Charlotte. This was not said in a spirit of criticism of his Bishop but merely as a statement of fact, for he also declared that he "preferred" to have his work given him. Throughout his long life of service he always had the feeling of doing a work assigned to him.

Cheshire quite naturally regretted leaving Chapel Hill, for he had been happy in his work there. He was also reluctant to part with his mission in Durham, which was created in a very real sense by his own labors. Recalling the first three years of his ministry, he declared: "I look upon my life at Chapel Hill as my pupilage, the completion of my training for my life work." [7]

CHAPTER III

Saint Peter's Parish

Cheshire entered upon his work in Charlotte with a feeling that here he had an excellent opportunity for extending the influence of his church, particularly in the missionary field. He did not feel any fear or trepidation at the thought of this larger and more difficult work, although he had no great confidence in his own ability. He went to his new parish with the determination to give to it his best, and throughout his rectorate there he never lost sight of that ideal. When some of his friends heard that he was going to St. Peter's, they told him he was taking over one of the hardest and most undesirable parishes in the Diocese. This was indeed a discouraging description of his new work, but after serving twelve years at St. Peter's, Cheshire remarked that he had found nothing which would justify such a characterization of that parish.

Cheshire did not bring his wife and children to Charlotte at once but left them in Chapel Hill for the summer. During this time he lived with Mr. John Wilkes, the senior warden of the parish, and took his meals at a boarding house. Finding no parish rectory in Charlotte, he bought a house on North Church Street. This purchase took all he had saved from his law practice, plus an additional thousand dollars which he had to borrow. His salary from St. Peter's being twelve hundred dollars a year, he was able to carry a debt of this amount. With a salary this size he felt that he had been "raised to a condition of affluence." In an exuberance of generosity he offered to become responsible for the support of an orphan in one of the foreign mission orphanages. For some reason his proposal was not accepted. It was not long, however, before he found that his salary was little if any above his actual needs.

When Cheshire became rector of St. Peter's there were one hundred and thirty-seven communicants in the parish. Mr. John Wilkes and Colonel Hamilton C. Jones were his senior and junior wardens, respectively. These men were quite different in temperament, but both were sincerely devoted to the welfare of the church. The young rector found in them staunch friends and helpful advisors. One of the first tasks Cheshire set for himself was to visit and become acquainted with each member of his congregation. After making a careful study of the parish register, he purchased a small memorandum book in which he wrote down the full name, age, and church status of each person connected with St. Peter's. By the end of his first summer in Charlotte he had become fairly well acquainted with most of his parishioners.

One of Cheshire's predecessors at St. Peter's was the Rev. Benjamin S. Bronson, rector of the parish from 1867 to 1878. He had been greatly interested in institutional work, and had begun several enterprises in the

Saint Peter's Parish

course of his ministry in Charlotte. None of these, however, was carried to a successful conclusion under his direction. Mr. Bronson's capacity seemed to be limited to merely initiating worth-while projects. His efforts were not futile, for he instilled in his congregation a deep interest in this type of work. Cheshire often said that what he was able to accomplish in Charlotte was due in part to the enthusiasm for institutional work which Mr. Bronson had aroused in his parishioners. He confessed that he did not have the type of mind which readily produced original ideas: "I think I can only methodize and put into practice ideas I get from others."[1] Although he exaggerated his lack of originality, he was strikingly successful in taking a good idea or suggestion and making it work.

When Cheshire came to Charlotte he found one of Mr. Bronson's charities still in existence, although in a sadly neglected condition. This was a four-room house which was known as St. Peter's Home and Hospital. The good work which was being done in a very small way by this institution strongly appealed to Cheshire. He regularly visited the sick there, and soon began to lay plans for enlarging its usefulness. For this purpose he enlisted the aid of a retired clergyman, Rev. Lucian Holmes, who was then conducting in Charlotte a small school for boys. Mr. Holmes visited the people of the city, soliciting contributions ranging from ten cents to one dollar a month. His efforts were successful, and in a comparatively short time the little hospital was assured of a modest monthly income. It was planned that the women on the Board of Managers of the hospital should collect the pledges. Thus, under Cheshire's direction, St.

Peter's hospital was firmly established and has continued to grow in usefulness to the community from that time to the present day.

Shortly after becoming rector of St. Peter's, Cheshire began to take an active interest in the church's work among the Negroes. He found among a large Negro population only one communicant. Prior to the Civil War Negroes had worshiped with the whites, sitting in galleries erected for their use. Following the war and reconstruction, however, the church had of necessity been forced to curtail its work among the Negroes. He recognized in this condition an opportunity for a great work. Since his parish was large and demanded the greater part of his time, he asked Bishop Lyman to send him an unmarried clergyman who could devote all his efforts to the Negro work. The Bishop complied with his request, and in the spring of 1882 sent Rev. Charles C. Quin to Charlotte. Quin received a stipend of two hundred dollars a year from the Diocese, which Cheshire supplemented with fifty dollars out of his own pocket. In addition, Quin lived with the Cheshires, who gave him his room and board.

After securing an assistant for the Negro work, Cheshire's next step was to find a place in which to worship. He found an old house in the Negro section of Charlotte, which he bought and remodeled sufficiently to make it serve as a mission. He named the little chapel St. Michael and All Angels. Although Quin was placed in charge of this mission, Cheshire held an evening service there every second Sunday. In this way he was able to keep in personal contact with the congregation.

The work progressed so well that it was not long before the need for a larger church was apparent. Seeing this need, Cheshire solicited contributions for a new church from his parishioners and from various churchmen throughout the Diocese. He sent Quin to Pennsylvania, New York, and Connecticut with letters to his friends in those states, asking for assistance. Cheshire and Quin were fairly successful in their efforts to raise funds for the new church, and in the spring of 1883 the cornerstone was laid. In the course of the year the nave and chancel were completed, while the transepts were left to be finished at some future time. It was a well-built brick church and large enough to allow for considerable growth in the congregation. It stands today as a testimonial to Cheshire's zeal in advancing the work of the church. Shortly after it was built, Quin resigned and was succeeded by Rev. Primus P. Alston, a colored clergyman, who remained in charge of the parish for over twenty years. St. Michael and All Angels was now practically independent of St. Peter's, although it was still under Cheshire's general direction.

While in the process of establishing St. Michael's, Cheshire was at the same time engaged in another missionary enterprise. He found in a section of Charlotte, known as Mechanicsville, a number of families who were members of the Episcopal Church but were not connected with St. Peter's parish. Seeing an opportunity to extend the work of the parish, he determined to bring the services of the church to these people. He began by establishing a Sunday school in an abandoned schoolhouse in this section. The Sunday school gradually expanded into a little mission, which he called St. Martin's. Not long after the mission was started, the building in which the services were held was destroyed by fire. Not permitting this misfortune to discourage him, he began almost at once to lay plans for the erection of a chapel on the same location.

After negotiating with the Charlotte school board, he was able to buy the property for fifteen hundred dollars, to be paid in three installments. Cheshire himself paid the first installment of five hundred dollars, while two of his parishioners guaranteed the remainder. He procured his part of the cost by selling a lot in Tarboro which his father had given him. When the land was bought, he began the work of raising money for the erection of a chapel. His loyal friend, Mr. John Wilkes, came forward as usual and supported him generously with both time and money. Other friends came to his assistance, and work was soon started on the building. Cheshire organized the Guild of St. Martin to help him in carrying forward the work on the chapel. Some time before it was completed, he began to hold a service in the little church every Sunday night. This service was in addition to three others which he held each Sunday at St. Peter's. Thus, Cheshire had literally built from the ground up the mission of St. Martin's. It maintained a steady growth and in time became one of the larger parishes of the Diocese.

There seems to have been almost no limit to Cheshire's missionary fervor. He was not content to confine his labors to the bounds of Charlotte. Shortly after coming to St. Peter's he visited Monroe, and there he found a number of churchmen who at one time had been served by the rector at Wadesboro. At the request of these churchmen Cheshire gave them a monthly service, being assisted for a time by Mr. Quin. In 1885 the work at Monroe was turned over to Rev. Edwin A. Osborne. During his rectorate at St. Peter's Cheshire also held

Saint Peter's Parish

services from time to time at Rockingham, Mooresville, Mount Mourne, and Davidson College. He did not, however, succeed in establishing a permanent mission at any one of these places. If he had had more time to devote to this distant missionary work, he might have met with better success.

In the fall of 1883 there came to Cheshire an opportunity to do what he later characterized as "the most entirely gratifying and successful work of all my missionary undertakings." [2] Columbus W. McCoy, of Long Creek Township, Mecklenburg County, invited Cheshire to hold a service in his community, stating that a number of people in his neighborhood had manifested an interest in the Episcopal Church. McCoy had formerly been a Presbyterian, but having become acquainted with the Book of Common Prayer, he expressed a desire to join the Episcopal Church. Cheshire accepted the invitation, and on November 18 held his first service there in the community schoolhouse. He passed the night with Mr. McCoy and spent the next day in visiting the people of the neighborhood. He felt that "very little can be accomplished in a new field by merely having a service, even a Sunday service, unless time is given to personal familiar visiting from house to house, to know the people, and to establish some influence among them." [3] He held a second service that night, and returned to Charlotte the following morning. This same procedure was followed in his subsequent visits.

In December Cheshire went again to Long Creek, but in consequence of bad weather, he did not return again until the spring. Beginning in May, 1884, he held monthly services in the Long Creek community. Observing the growing interest of the community in the church, he decided to hold a series of services for them from August 12 through the 16th. He secured the assistance of Rev. Dr. George B. Wetmore and Rev. Mr. Osborne. The services were held in Beach Cliff Schoolhouse and were so well attended that part of the congregation was forced to sit out-of-doors. Cheshire and his assistants took turns in preaching in the morning and evening. In the afternoons they visited those families who had shown an interest in becoming members of the church. In the course of the week they baptized sixteen persons, for the most part children, and at the end of the services fourteen adults signified their desire to be confirmed. At the close of the week's preaching Cheshire was presented with a petition signed by eleven persons who asked that they be organized as a mission under the name of St. Mark's Chapel. This was indeed a successful conclusion to the week's work.

On October 25 Bishop Lyman visited Long Creek and confirmed sixteen persons. Following the confirmation he organized the congregation as a mission to be known as St. Mark's. Cheshire continued his monthly visits to the new mission until January, 1885, at which time he turned this work over to Rev. Edwin A. Osborne, who had already taken charge of Cheshire's congregation in Monroe. Upon assuming this work Mr. Osborne moved from Henderson County to Charlotte. During the remainder of Cheshire's rectorate at St. Peter's, he and Mr. Osborne became intimate friends and co-operated generously in each other's work.

Although Cheshire devoted most of his time and energy to St. Peter's parish and its missions, he did not neglect his duty to the Diocese. He attended all of the diocesan conventions and took an active and significant part in their deliberations. Probably the most important action taken by any convention during his ministry was that relating to the division of the Diocese. The question of dividing the church in North Carolina into two dioceses had been discussed from time to time by the conventions since the election in 1873 of Bishop Lyman as assistant bishop. Bishop Atkinson had favored a division at one time, but when the question was placed squarely before the convention of 1877, he came out strongly against it. The large number of clergy and laity who favored division dropped the proposal for the time-being out of deference to Bishop Atkinson, who, they felt, did not have much longer to serve. Upon his death in January, 1881, the question was again brought forward. At the convention of 1882, held in Calvary Church, Tarboro, Dr. M. M. Marshall, rector of Christ Church, Raleigh, introduced resolutions declaring the sentiment of the people on division and calling for a committee to consider proposals for the erection of a new diocese. The convention approved Dr. Marshall's resolutions, and the Bishop appointed a special committee to report upon the subject.

After some study of the proposal this committee submitted a majority report calling for a division of the Diocese. Bishop Lyman, who during Bishop Atkinson's life-time had advocated the formation of a new diocese, now reversed his position. Upon hearing the report of the special committee, the Bishop delivered "an impassioned attack upon the report."[4] The opposition of the Bishop led to a long and, at times, acrimonious discussion. When the question was finally voted upon, the committee's report was adopted by a large majority of the clergy and laity. The convention appointed a committee of clergymen and laymen to confer with the Bishop upon the details of the division, to obtain his consent, and to report to the next diocesan convention. Cheshire was made a member of this committee.

St. Peter's parish, Charlotte, was host to the diocesan convention of 1883. The most pressing and important business of this convention was the question of forming a new diocese. On the second day the Committee on Conference with the Bishop made its report. The committee stated that after a consultation with the Bishop it found that he was opposed to a division of the Diocese because he felt that one bishop in good health could do the work for the entire state, and that the church in North Carolina was not financially able to support two bishops and two diocesan organizations. The Bishop told the committee, however, that he would consent to the erection of a new diocese provided a large majority of clergy and laity desired it, the line of division to be satisfactory to him, and the permanent funds to be divided equally between the two dioceses. Following the report the convention voted on the question: forty-two clergymen voted for division, and eleven against; twenty-nine parishes voted for, and ten against. Cheshire voted for the creation of a new diocese, as he had done in the convention the year before.

When the question of a territorial division came up for discussion, Cheshire moved that the new diocese be composed of the counties of Hertford, Bertie, Martin, Pitt, Greene, Wayne, Sampson, Cumberland, and Robeson, and all that part of the state located between those counties and the Atlantic coast. Cheshire later withdrew his motion when the special Committee on a Line of Division presented an amended report which embodied in sub-

Saint Peter's Parish

stance his recommendation. The convention unanimously adopted the amended report. Cheshire was in favor of placing the counties of Edgecombe and Halifax in the eastern Diocese and retaining Cumberland in the old Diocese. When he saw, however, that Bishop Lyman would not give up Edgecombe and Halifax, he recommended that Cumberland should be included in the new division. This was the arrangement finally adopted.

After an agreement had been reached on the line of demarcation, Cheshire offered the following resolutions: (1) that the convention of 1883 ratify the work of the convention of 1882 relative to a division of the Diocese; (2) that the Bishop of the Diocese and the General Convention of the church be requested to give their consent to this procedure; and (3) that all the securities and properties of the church in North Carolina be equally divided between the two dioceses, as should be agreed upon by a committee representing both. Cheshire's resolutions were voted upon separately, and were all adopted. Following their approval the convention received a letter from Bishop Lyman announcing his consent to the formation of a new diocese. Thus was decided an important, and vexing, problem of the church in North Carolina.

The convention of 1883 was the first in which Cheshire had taken a significant part, but from that time forward his influence and counsel became increasingly important. He was made chairman of the committee on the division of diocesan properties. His committee had a difficult task in dividing the permanent funds of the church to the satisfaction of both dioceses. The problem caused a few very bitter discussions in several succeeding conventions. Cheshire usually led the discussions, often taking the side of the new diocese against Bishop

Lyman and a majority in the convention. More often than not he won his point, since his opponents rarely took the pains to make themselves fully acquainted with the facts. Cheshire was sometimes accused of being discourteous in his manner towards the Bishop when they disagreed. It can be fairly said, however, that he was never intentionally so. In a letter to the Bishop he remarked that he often spoke excitedly and impetuously upon any subject about which he felt very strongly, and that this characteristic was sometimes interpreted as discourtesy.[5] Cheshire had the highest respect for Bishop Lyman and admired him both as a bishop and a man. Nevertheless, it was almost inevitable that two such decided and forthright characters as Lyman and Cheshire should have pronounced disagreements.

One of Cheshire's most valuable contributions to the diocesan conventions was his services on the Committee on Canons. He was a member of this committee from 1884 through 1893, with the exception of 1887–88, serving as its chairman for several years. He made himself thoroughly acquainted with the canons of the church, and while serving on the committee, he did most of its work. During these years debates on the canons occupied much of the time of the annual conventions. Long after becoming bishop, Cheshire remarked that he was happy to observe that this was no longer true, and that "We have come to be interested in more important business." He did not mean to belittle the value of canonical law, but rather to emphasize the importance of other work.

In 1887 Cheshire made a revision of the canons, expecting the convention of that year to call for a revisal. He also carefully annotated the canons and the articles of the diocesan constitution. The convention of 1887 did call for a revision to be made and be presented to it the next year. However, Cheshire was "surprised and disappointed" when the Bishop did not reappoint him to the Committee on Canons. Hearing of the work Cheshire had already done on the canons, Dr. Kemp P. Battle suggested that he should present to the next convention his revision as a substitute for the one to be proposed by the committee. Cheshire decided to follow this suggestion. When the committee presented its report to the convention of 1888, he rose to say that he had prepared a revision of the canons the year before and had been advised by some of his friends to offer it as a substitute. Several requests were made from the floor that he should explain his work. Following his explanation a motion was made that his revisal be adopted in place of that of the Committee on Canons. The motion was carried by a large majority, and after making several minor changes, the convention adopted Cheshire's revision. Its action was a signal tribute to the high character of Cheshire's work.

From time to time Cheshire served on other regular and special committees. He was a member of the Executive Missionary Committee from 1885 to 1891, and a member of the Board of Managers of the Thompson Orphanage from 1886 through 1893. In all his activities he manifested a zealous interest in the affairs of the Diocese. In consequence of his work in the diocesan conventions and his productive ministry in Charlotte, he came to be recognized as one of the outstanding clergymen of the state.

Cheshire's first personal contact with the work of the church outside of North Carolina was with the University of the South at Sewanee, Tennessee. Feeling that the churchmen of his Diocese displayed an unwarrantable lack of interest in the welfare of the University of the South, he resolved to bring to their attention the needs and opportunities of the institution. In 1885 he made an appeal for support of the school in the columns of the *Church Messenger*. He wrote personal letters to prominent churchmen, and made addresses on behalf of the University in as many parishes as he could conveniently reach. His voluntary efforts met with some success. Perceiving Cheshire's active interest in the school, Dr. Jarvis Buxton, clerical trustee for the University from the Diocese of North Carolina, resigned this position at the convention of 1885. Dr. Buxton then nominated Cheshire to succeed him, and the convention unanimously confirmed his nomination. From 1887 until he was elected bishop he attended every meeting of the trustees. During this period Cheshire formed many lasting friendships with the trustees and professors he met at Sewanee. These associations gave him a better understanding of the church's work outside of his Diocese.

The diocesan convention further recognized Cheshire's ability by electing him one of the clerical deputies to the Triennial General Convention of 1886. He was re-elected a deputy to the succeeding conventions of 1889 and 1892. As far as the journals reveal, he did not take an active part in any of these meetings. It was characteristic of him to have little to say in a body of which he was a new member until he had become thoroughly acquainted with its personnel and procedure. At the General Convention of 1889 he was made a member of the Missionary Council and was re-elected to the Council in 1892. Attendance upon these conventions further broadened his knowledge of the work of the

Saint Peter's Parish 41

national church and brought him into contact with many of its prominent figures.

In consequence of his energetic parochial work and his active participation in diocesan affairs, Cheshire received, during his rectorate at St. Peter's, several calls to other parishes. In September, 1888, the vestry of Calvary Church, Tarboro, asked him to become their rector to succeed his father, who wished to retire. Cheshire refused the call. It is to be supposed that he preferred the larger opportunities offered in Charlotte, but his personal papers do not reveal why he rejected the invitation. Writing to him concerning his refusal, Bishop Lyman stated that he was pleased to learn that Cheshire was to remain in Charlotte, and that he recognized "how great a calamity it would have been to the interest of the Church, in your own, and in the adjacent counties, had you decided to resign your present position. I am sure, too, that your determination to remain will greatly strengthen the hearts of those around you, and greatly increase your powers of usefulness." [6] This commendation of his work by Bishop Lyman, who was not inclined to give excessive praise, must have been encouraging to Cheshire. Three years later he received a call from the vestry of St. Paul's Church, Macon, Georgia. They offered him a rectory and a salary of sixteen hundred dollars a year, but he also declined this call.

The most complimentary consideration Cheshire received, prior to 1893, was in the summer of 1891. At that time Rev. Henry Lucas, rector of St. Mark's Church, Brunswick, Georgia, in behalf of himself and several other clergymen, wrote Cheshire to ask if he had any objection to his name being used as a nominee for bishop of Georgia. Lucas stated that the diocesan convention of Georgia was to meet on July 1, in Macon, to elect a bishop. Cheshire replied that if he were elected by the convention he would be "on the whole unwilling to accept." The Georgia convention met and elected a bishop, but Cheshire's name was not placed in nomination because the delegates did not wish to risk a refusal. Rev. A. W. Dodge, a member of the convention, wrote Cheshire: "I think we could have elected you without any great difficulty if you had been willing to serve us." [7] In none of his writings examined does Cheshire give an explanation of his unwillingness to become bishop of Georgia. His love for North Carolina and its people and a sincere conviction that he should devote his life to the work of the church in this state is probably the best explanation of his decision.

During these years in which Cheshire was assuming a greater share of diocesan work, his parochial and missionary duties in and outside of Charlotte were not neglected. The only serious criticism of his services which was brought to his attention by his parishioners was that the missions in Iredell and Mecklenburg counties demanded too much of his time. Cheshire, however, maintained that in serving the rural missions he was at the same time building up St. Peter's, since the missions would eventually furnish many new members to the town parish. In spite of this criticism, he continued his missionary and institutional work. In 1885 and 1886 he gave wholehearted assistance to Rev. Edwin A. Osborne in establishing the Thompson Orphanage in Charlotte as a diocesan institution. The last parochial enterprise of St. Peter's Church in which he participated was the founding of the Good Samaritan Hospital for Negroes. The movement for the hospital was initiated by Mrs.

Saint Peter's Parish 43

John Wilkes, with whom Cheshire co-operated in every way. He devoted much time to raising the money for the purchase of a lot. In 1888 he laid the cornerstone of the hospital and three years later officiated at its formal opening. The Good Samaritan was the first hospital for Negroes to be established in North Carolina.

In the course of his pastorate in Charlotte Cheshire was on the friendliest of terms with the ministers of the other denominations, although he sometimes strongly differed with them. He was a member of the local Ministerial Association, serving for a time as its vice-president. The association often passed resolutions inviting popular preachers to hold revivals in Charlotte. Cheshire, not in sympathy with professional revivalists, customarily opposed this procedure.

When the association once invited the well-known preacher, Sam Jones, to hold a series of services in Charlotte for ten days, all the ministers except Cheshire closed their churches during the revival. At the time, he was criticized rather severely for his lack of co-operation. Some eighteen months later Jones announced he was returning for a second revival, although he had received no invitation. Hearing of his plans, the Baptist pastor, at the next meeting of the Ministerial Association, proposed a resolution that the ministers of the town should not close their churches during Jones' visit, nor co-operate with him. He declared that, while his church had gained a good many members immediately following the revivalist's services, most of them had by this time deserted him, and the whole effect of Jones' preaching had been to lower and demoralize the religious life of his congregation. The other ministers concurred in his opinion. Cheshire, however, objected to the resolution on the grounds that he would not oppose any man who, as far as he knew, was "honestly trying to preach the Gospel as he understood it." He opposed it also as a matter of policy, since, in his opinion, nothing would please Jones more than to be able to say that "a lot of little two-by-four preachers got together, and voted to keep Sam Jones out of Charlotte." [8] Cheshire's argument convinced the other clergymen that he was right, and the resolution was dropped. The incident well illustrates his keen sense of fairness and good judgment.

Cheshire's domestic and social life in Charlotte was happy and interesting. Although his salary was not large, he was able to make his family reasonably comfortable. When he and Mrs. Cheshire left Chapel Hill, they had two children, Elizabeth and Sarah. During their twelve years in Charlotte four other children were born to them—Joseph Blount, Annie, Godfrey, and James Webb. This was a large family to support on a clergyman's salary, but by good management they were able to make their life pleasant. The Cheshires were hospitable people and enjoyed entertaining their friends. The Dean of the Convocation of Charlotte and the Diocesan Evangelist, as well as many other visiting clergymen, usually stayed with them when visiting St. Peter's parish.

Cheshire made many friends in Charlotte outside of his congregation as well as among his parishioners. He accomplished a great deal in building up a more friendly attitude on the part of the other denominations towards the Episcopal Church. The fearless and positive stand he always took on questions involving the principles and policies of his church, while antagonizing some people for a time, in the end won him many admirers and the respect of all.

Saint Peter's Parish 45

When Cheshire resigned his rectorate of St. Peter's in 1893 to become assistant bishop of the Diocese of North Carolina, he left in the parish a record difficult for any future rector to equal. In the course of his twelve years at St. Peter's he had increased its membership from one hundred and thirty-seven to two hundred and sixty-three. He organized and established St. Martin's parish, St. Michael and All Angels' mission for Negroes, St. Mark's mission at Mecklenburg, and St. Paul's mission at Monroe. He sponsored the building of St. Peter's and the Good Samaritan hospitals, and assisted Rev. E. A. Osborne in establishing the Thompson Orphanage. These were significant accomplishments for a rectorate of twelve years. But as almost everyone else, Cheshire also experienced some failures. In his attempts to establish missions at Rockingham, Mooresville, and Mount Mourne, he had not been successful. However, balanced against his successes, these failures seem small.

CHAPTER IV

Election to the Episcopate

Theodore Benedict Lyman was elected assistant bishop of North Carolina in 1873, and upon the death of Bishop Thomas Atkinson in 1881 he assumed the control of the Diocese. In 1891 he celebrated in Christ Church, Raleigh, the fiftieth anniversary of his ordination to the priesthood. By this time the Bishop had begun to show signs that the duties of his office were becoming too arduous for his failing strength. It was not until two years later, however, that he felt that he must ask for assistance in his Episcopal duties. When the diocesan convention met in Christ Church, Raleigh, on May 17, 1893, Bishop Lyman brought to the attention of the body his failing health and the necessity of conserving his strength. He stated he would welcome any suggestions on the subject the convention saw fit to make. The subject of assisting the Bishop was taken under consideration immediately, and a committee was appointed to study how best this might be accomplished.

The following day this committee recommended, in the form of several resolutions, that Bishop Lyman should be relieved of a part of his official work by the election of an assistant bishop; that when the convention completed its present session it should adjourn to meet again in Raleigh on June 27 to elect an assistant bishop; and that the present convention should take steps towards determining a salary for the new office. The resolutions were adopted in their entirety.

Before taking up the proceedings of the adjourned convention, it is interesting to consider here some views Cheshire once expressed on the Episcopate in North Carolina. In 1891 a friend wrote him asking who he thought would make a good successor to Bishop Lyman. In reply to this query, Cheshire remarked that he did not approve of anyone's expressing an arbitrary opinion as to the choice of a bishop for this Diocese, but since that was what his friend desired, he would offer some suggestions. He declared that Dr. Francis J. Murdoch, Rector of St. Luke's, Salisbury, was his first choice, and characterized him as a learned, noble, and lovable man. His second and third choices were the Rev. Robert S. Barrett, of Atlanta, and the Rev. Mr. Winchester, of Nashville. Above everything, said Cheshire, "We want a plain man—one who can come down to the plain people of our country." He did not suggest anyone above the age of fifty, since he thought it was better to choose a clergyman "rather under than above his prime." Speaking in general of the election of bishops, Cheshire observed: "I really, and in all seriousness, think that there is something providential in the choice of a man to the office of Bishop. The best men are so often those who were hardly thought of beforehand—sometimes hardly heard of."[1] To illustrate his point, he cited the elections of Bishops Ravenscroft, of North Carolina, Whipple, of Minnesota, and Jackson, of Alabama. These observations are particularly interesting, coming as they did only two years before the proposed election of an assistant bishop.

When the adjourned convention convened in Christ Church on June 27, Bishop Lyman gave his canonical consent to the election of an assistant bishop. The convention then provided that the new office should carry with it an annual salary of twenty-five hundred dollars.

At the afternoon session the doors of the convention were closed, and nominations for an assistant bishop by the clergy were in order. The clergymen nominated were Rev. Nathaniel H. Harding, Dr. Joseph Blount Cheshire, Jr., Rev. T. M. N. George, Dr. Francis J. Murdoch, Dr. Matthias M. Marshall, and Rev. Robert S. Barrett. It is significant that all of these candidates, with the exception of R. S. Barrett, of Atlanta, were clergymen resident in North Carolina. It is also of interest that Murdoch and Cheshire, who were to be the two most important candidates, nominated each other. In his nomination speech Dr. Murdoch said: "The good shepherd knows his sheep. This is pre-eminently true of Dr. Cheshire. He knows the people of North Carolina, their history, their relationships, better perhaps than any other person living." [2]

Under the rules of the convention the clergy elects a bishop by a two-thirds vote of their number. Their choice is then submitted to the laity, who either ratify or reject it. In this convention twenty-nine votes was the necessary majority for election.

On the first three ballots, although all candidates received some votes, Cheshire led each time. But after the third ballot, the contest was narrowed down to Cheshire, Barrett, and Murdoch. Cheshire remained ahead through the sixth ballot; Murdoch then took the lead, which he

Election to the Episcopate 49

held, with the exception of five ballots, through the twenty-fourth. During this balloting, Barrett led all candidates twice and tied with Murdoch for the highest number three times. After the twenty-fourth ballot Cheshire asked to be excused from further attendance. He explained that he had expected the convention to last only one day and had accordingly promised to marry a friend on the twenty-eighth.* He was excused, and without further balloting the convention adjourned at eleven-thirty in the evening.

The following morning balloting was resumed, with Murdoch continuing to hold his lead. On the twenty-ninth ballot the Rev. Arthur S. Lloyd, of Norfolk, Virginia, was nominated and remained in the contest until the end. From the thirty-second through the thirty-fifth ballots Cheshire did not receive a single vote; while from the thirty-sixth through the thirty-eighth he received only one vote on each. Before the thirty-seventh was taken, Rev. W. S. Barrows moved that if no one was elected within the next two ballots, the clergy should retire from the convention for a conference. His motion was carried. Since no election took place, the clergy repaired to Christ Church chapel for prayer and conference.

There was a small minority in the convention, numbering ten or twelve clergymen, who were opposed to electing anyone from the Diocese of North Carolina. This minority held the balance between the stronger candidates and thus prevented an election. All attempts to compromise with the minority on some candidate other than Murdoch or Cheshire failed. Thereupon, when the

---

* Dr. Stephen B. Weeks was the friend Cheshire referred to. The wedding took place in Randolph County.

clergy met in the chapel, it was agreed that they should arrive at a choice by the process of elimination. After several votes were taken, the selection lay between Cheshire and Murdoch. The supporters of both men then agreed to vote in the convention for the one who received the highest vote in this conference. When the votes were counted, it was found that Cheshire led by a majority of one. The clergy then re-entered the church and took the thirty-ninth ballot, which resulted in twenty-nine votes for Cheshire, seven for Lloyd, and five scattered. The laity quickly confirmd the choice of the clergy by a vote of twenty-four to seven; whereupon the Bishop declared Rev. Joseph Blount Cheshire, Jr., elected assistant bishop of the Diocese and appointed a committee to notify him of his election.

After performing the promised marriage ceremony, Cheshire went to High Point to spend the night. When he arrived, he found several telegrams from friends congratulating him upon his election. Describing his reaction to the news, he said that he "could not comprehend what they meant, and thought there must be some mistake. I was more deeply agitated than I could have anticipated." The following day he wrote his father: "The one thing in the election at Raleigh which gives me unmixed satisfaction is the knowledge that it would be a happiness to you and to mother. In every other respect my feelings are of so confused a kind that I hardly know myself what to do or say.... I feel that this election has its human cause and origin in your life-long labor for the church, and in the name and good will of our people which I have derived from you and not made for myself." [3] This sincere statement of his thoughts about his election was characteristic of Cheshire. He felt profoundly the great

Election to the Episcopate 51

responsibility which had been placed upon him, and wrote a friend that he could never have undertaken it had he not felt that he had the "sympathy, co-operation, and prayer" [4] of his people.

The month following his election Cheshire received more than two hundred letters and telegrams of congratulation. They came from clergymen and laymen in and outside of North Carolina, and a great many were from persons who were not members of the Episcopal Church. One of the most common sentiments found in these letters was the pleasure and gratification expressed at the election of a North Carolinian as assistant bishop. It is a noteworthy fact that Cheshire was the first native clergyman of the state to be elected to the Episcopate of the Diocese of North Carolina.

Dr. Francis J. Murdoch, as well as many of his adherents, sent their sincere congratulations. In a circular letter to his supporters, thanking them for their efforts in his behalf, Dr. Murdoch said of Cheshire: "The election has ended as I wished. Other men may tremble as to the outcome. I have not one misgiving. Neither love for Dr. Cheshire nor prejudice against any man can warp my judgment in this matter. I say now (as I said when I nominated him) that we have made no mistake." [5] This warm praise from a man of Dr. Murdoch's high character and ability must have been very encouraging to Cheshire.

An amusing and interesting tribute to Cheshire's election as assistant bishop were some verses by Rev. John E. C. Smedes. Dr. Smedes, a former clergyman of the Diocese, had been one of Cheshire's examiners for deacon's orders and had presented him for ordination as priest. His lines are as follows:

CONGRATULATIONS TO A BISHOP-ELECT

News sweeter and fresher
I ask not, Joe Cheshire:
You are bishop assistant
Elect; though too distant
For love's fondest issue,
Alas! or I'd kiss you.
'Twas my joy to examine you
And find no mean sham in you;
For deep did they ram in you,
At Berkeley and Trinity,
A full charge of divinity.
'Twas my joy, mine eye feasted,
To see duly priested
The youth I presented.
And now I'm contented:
They will make you a bishop.
I send a meek wish up
To the Shepherd above,
That in wisdom and love
You may long feed His sheep,
While the Faith you still keep,
And then, crosier laid down,
May at last wear a crown.

Shortly after his election Cheshire received an invitation from the vestry of Calvary Church, Tarboro, to have his consecration service held there. He accepted the invitation and selected October 15 as the date. It was indeed fitting that he should be consecrated in the church which his father had served for a half century and in which he himself had been brought up and ordained to the diaconate.

On the day of Cheshire's consecration the little town

Election to the Episcopate 53

of Tarboro was taxed almost to its capacity to take care of the out-of-town people who had come for the service. About thirty clergymen from the dioceses of North Carolina and East Carolina were present. The service began at eleven in the morning. The ecclesiastical procession, headed by seven bishops and the bishop-elect, entered the church singing the hymn "The Church's One Foundation." Rt. Rev. T. U. Dudley, Bishop of Kentucky, preached the sermon. Bishop Lyman was the consecrator, assisted by Bishops Watson, of East Carolina, and Capers, of South Carolina. Cheshire was presented by Bishop Weed, of Florida, and Bishop Sessums, of Louisiana. The venerable Bishop Quintard, of Tennessee, also took part in the service. All of the bishops joined in the laying on of hands. During the service the choir sang the anthem "How Beautiful upon the Mountains are the Feet of Them that Publish Good Tidings," composed by Rev. Dr. M. A. Curtis. It is interesting to note that this anthem was sung at the ordination of Dr. J. B. Cheshire, Sr., in 1840 and at the ordination of Rev. J. B. Cheshire, Jr., in 1880. The service closed with the singing of the recessional "Holy, Holy, Holy." It was a beautiful and impressive ceremony, but its beauty was marred for Cheshire by the absence of his father, who was not well enough to attend.

Bishop Cheshire's first episcopal act was to hold an evening service in Tarboro, the night of his consecration, at St. Luke's Chapel for Negroes. He did not lose any time in assuming the duties of his new office. While in Tarboro he made several visitations in Edgecombe and Halifax counties. On October 23 he and his family returned to Charlotte, but he did not tarry long. A few days later he set out for the mountains of North Carolina, where he spent a month visiting the scattered churches and missions in that section. Returning from the mountains, he continued his visitations until he was suddenly called to Raleigh on December 13 by the death of Bishop Lyman, who had been in greatly enfeebled health for the past few months.

The death of Bishop Lyman placed the Assistant Bishop in full charge of the Diocese of North Carolina. The few weeks of work Bishop Cheshire had had under the direction and advice of the senior bishop stood him in good stead now that he had the sole responsibility for episcopal guidance of the Diocese.

CHAPTER V

First Years in the Episcopacy

When Bishop Cheshire assumed the episcopal oversight of the Diocese of North Carolina, he felt little confidence in his ability to fulfill the duties of the office. He did feel that by sincere and diligent application he could accomplish much for the welfare of the church. When elected assistant bishop he was, in his own words, "constrained to accept the call, not from any sense of fitness in myself, but simply because such a call seems to me to carry with it an imperative obligation to accept, unless the hand of God should plainly point in another direction: a dispensation was laid upon me." [1] Notwithstanding his expressed views, Bishop Cheshire was, in the opinion of most churchmen, better fitted for his office by ability, temperament, and training than any other man in North Carolina.

Bishop Cheshire met his first diocesan convention in May, 1894, at St. Paul's Church, Winston. He opened his annual address by saying: "I cannot bring into any order or method in my own mind, much less can I put it into words, the feelings which this occasion calls up. To no one can it seem stranger than it does to myself that I should occupy this place, and thus address you from the chair of Ravenscroft, of Atkinson, and of him so lately taken from us." He made no recommendations for important changes in the policy or work of the church, since he wished to become more thoroughly acquainted with the problems and needs of the Diocese before doing so. The Bishop urged upon the clergy then, as he was to do many times in the future, the necessity of keeping their parochial records in proper order, and observed that no businessman would employ a clerk for a week if he kept his books as many of the parish registers were kept. In concluding his address, the Bishop touched on three subjects which were to be collectively the theme of his episcopate: namely, the importance of regarding the Diocese rather than the parish as the unit of the church; the necessity of supporting all diocesan institutions; and the great need for continuing and expanding the missionary work of the Diocese. Time and time again he drove home the spirit and essence of these subjects, until the clergy and laity alike caught some of the fire of his enthusiasm and translated his ideas into living reality.

One of the first diocesan projects Bishop Cheshire undertook was the revival of the old mission of Valle Crucis, established by Bishop Ives about fifty years before. At the same time he planned to revive the mission work along the Watauga River. For this difficult work the Bishop had one man in mind who he thought was eminently qualified—Rev. Milnor Jones. His first meeting with Jones had been at the convention of 1883. Shortly afterwards, Bishop Lyman had asked Cheshire if he would carry to Jones a sum of money which had been raised to aid him in erecting a church at Tryon. The Bishop had added that he hoped Cheshire would spend a few days with Jones to observe his work. Cheshire complied with

First Years in the Episcopacy 57

the Bishop's request, and spent a few unforgettable days with Jones, driving with him over the hills and valleys of Polk County to visit his scattered missions. At the time, he had been greatly impressed with Jones' influence with the mountain people. When he began to plan the revival of Valle Crucis, he remembered his experience with the picturesque mountain missionary.

Milnor Jones, however, was in Oregon when the Bishop was ready to commence his mountain work. In January, 1894, Cheshire wrote asking him to return to North Carolina. In replying to Bishop Cheshire, Jones wrote this characteristically laconic letter: "Where do you want me to go? What do you wish me to do? And what salary will you give? Not that the *amount* of the salary makes any difference; I only wish to know just what I have to go on." The Bishop answered as concisely: "I want you to go to Valle Crucis, on the Watauga River. I want you to revive the old Valle Crucis Mission, as your special work; and I give you for your field of operations Watauga, Mitchell, and Ashe Counties, to do what you can in them. I will give you six hundred dollars a year, payable monthly." [2]

Milnor Jones was a rough, plain-spoken individual with a remarkable faculty for understanding and winning the confidence of the simple mountain folk. He had a deeply religious nature, and a complete fearlessness in preaching the Gospel as he understood it. Bishop Cheshire found him an unusually effective man in laying the foundations of missionary work, but from that point he seemed to lack the power to build further.

Jones entered with enthusiasm upon his work in the mountains of North Carolina. When the Bishop began his visitations to the western counties in June, 1895, he found that Jones had made a promising beginning. Bishop Cheshire spent several weeks with him, visiting one mission station after another in the counties of Mitchell, Watauga, and Ashe. They preached, baptized, and confirmed in the most out-of-the-way places and under the most varied conditions. When they first visited Bakersville they held services in the courthouse, but upon their return for a second service some time later, they were refused the use of the building on the grounds that the courthouse was not safe for large crowds. The local newspaper, however, gave as the reason for the refusal the fact that the Methodists and Baptists held that "the Episcopalians had been preaching uncomfortable doctrine." The Bishop and Jones were not to be daunted; they held their service on the street in front of the courthouse. A large congregation gathered for the service. When the Bishop began preaching he did not think his voice would reach the assemblage, but after a few minutes he felt as if he could make himself heard "a mile away." He afterwards declared that "I never spoke with more ease, freedom, and enjoyment, or with a greater sense of the high privilege of being a servant and ambassador of my Lord." [3]

Another interesting episode in Bishop Cheshire's mission work in the mountains took place at Beaver Creek, Ashe County, in the summer of 1896. Here the Bishop and Jones were maintaining a mission school with two teachers in a building which had been leased for two years. When the Bishop went to the schoolhouse to hold a service, he was met by a mob of more than fifty men who "forcibly prevented" him from entering. The mob declared that the reason they were preventing him from holding his service was that they did not like "Mr. Jones's doctrine" and they understood that he, the Bishop, taught the same doctrine. In reporting the incident to the convention of the Jurisdiction of Asheville, the Bishop described it as "an experience which I certainly had never thought a possibility in my native state of North Carolina." [4]

In reviving the old mission at Valle Crucis Bishop Cheshire did not intend to follow the plan of Bishop Ives, which had been to establish a boys' school and a training school for the clergy. His primary motive was to evangelize the people of the mountain counties. He wanted to make Valle Crucis "an associate mission from which preachers and teachers should go out and keep up the work of evangelizing, instructing, and educating wherever an opening might be found or made." [5]

Milnor Jones, carrying letters of introduction from his Bishop, in the fall of 1895 visited the northern states to raise funds for his mountain work. He was successful in his efforts and, with the money thus raised, mission schools were established at Valle Crucis and at Beaver Creek. In the course of 1896 and 1897 a mission home, consisting of an eight-room house, was erected at Valle Crucis at a cost of twelve hundred dollars. It was built to accommodate a missionary, a teacher, and several pupils attending the mission school. Shortly after this constructive beginning Milnor Jones gave up the work at Valle Crucis. He confined his efforts to the small mission stations scattered over Mitchell, Watauga, and Ashe counties. The Bishop placed Rev. Samuel F. Adams in charge of Valle Crucis, and under his guidance and that of his successors the work progressed steadily.

Milnor Jones left North Carolina towards the end of 1897. He, with the assistance and encouragement of

Bishop Cheshire, had laid the foundations of a missionary work which was to be a credit to the church. Referring once to the character of Jones' work, the Bishop remarked: "If I had a wild mountain country full of moonshiners, I think I would like to have him, but for anything more civilized he is too savage." [6] With all of Jones' crudeness and faults, Bishop Cheshire believed him to be "really a more Godly man than many an one whose life is perfectly conventional and blameless." The Bishop often remarked that the visits he made to Milnor Jones in the mountains of North Carolina were among the most interesting experiences of his career.

Coinciding with Bishop Cheshire's efforts to expand and revive the missionary work of the church in the mountains, a movement was initiated to create a missionary district from the western counties of the Diocese of North Carolina. At the diocesan convention of 1894 a committee was appointed to study the advisability of requesting the General Convention to organize the western counties of the state into a missionary jurisdiction. It was felt by many that the present Diocese was too large to be adequately administered and supervised by one bishop. In his address to the convention of 1895 Bishop Cheshire substantiated this view when he reported that during the past year he had been able to devote only nine weeks to the western section of the state, which embraced nearly thirty counties.

The Bishop was "in sentiment" strongly opposed to a division of his Diocese, for he disliked seeing the church in North Carolina divided further. Also, he had become deeply interested in his mountain missions and was loath to relinquish them. He realized, however, the impossibility of properly serving such a large territory. Moreover,

First Years in the Episcopacy 61

he was determined not to make the mistake which he thought Bishop Atkinson, in 1877, and Bishop Lyman, in 1882, had made when they opposed the formation of a new diocese. In his opinion, a bishop "makes a mistake, when he opposes the well-settled convictions of his clergy and people upon a matter affecting the development of the Diocese." [7]

When the diocesan convention met in May, 1895, the Committee on the Proposed Missionary Jurisdiction recommended that the General Convention be requested to set apart the western section of the Diocese of North Carolina as a missionary jurisdiction. It was further recommended that the line of division should be the eastern boundaries of the counties of Alleghany, Wilkes, Alexander, Catawba, Lincoln and Gaston. Bishop Cheshire had suggested to the committee this territorial division. Although it meant a great loss of strength to his own Diocese, the Bishop believed that the missionary jurisdiction should be made large enough to be of importance, and that it should be created with the view of its becoming a diocese at some future date. The convention adopted the committee's recommendations, and instructed its deputies to present them to the General Convention.

When this body met in the fall of 1895, Bishop Cheshire presented in the House of Bishops the memorial of the Diocese of North Carolina requesting the erection of a missionary jurisdiction. The memorial was referred to the Committee on Domestic Missions. A few days later the Bishop of Florida, chairman of the committee, reported the memorial unfavorably, stating that his committee did not believe the reasons set forth were sufficient to justify an affirmative action. He further reported that the legal and constitutional requirements had not been properly provided for. Bishop Cheshire then introduced a resolution calling for the erection of a missionary district and providing that it should be under the limited jurisdiction of the Bishop and Convention of the Diocese of North Carolina until such constitutional amendments could be adopted to remove the objections advanced by the Bishop of Florida. The House of Bishops adopted the resolution with little discussion, and two days later it was approved by the House of Deputies. Following this action Bishop Cheshire moved that the House of Bishops should proceed to the election of a missionary bishop for the newly created district. His motion met with opposition and was postponed to a future meeting of the House of Bishops. The district, which was to be known as the Jurisdiction of Asheville, was temporarily placed under the episcopal care of Bishop Cheshire.

Only a few weeks after the close of the General Convention, Bishop Cheshire, on November 12, 1895, met the first convention of the Missionary Jurisdiction of Asheville. He outlined to the clergy and laity what would be expected of them as a missionary jurisdiction, and gave much helpful advice on setting up the machinery for carrying on their work. The Bishop called to their attention the almost incalculable opportunities for extending the influence of the church in the mountain counties. The next year he greatly expanded this idea in a charge to the clergy of the Jurisdiction. The Bishop pointed out that nine-tenths of the work in the Jurisdiction of Asheville was to evangelize people who were almost wholly ignorant of the church. Such material aids as rectories, schoolhouses, and even churches, while undoubtedly helpful, were not necessary adjuncts to the primary object of the church: "to catch men." He urged the

First Years in the Episcopacy 63

clergy to know the people, to preach to them in words they could understand, and to make religion an integral part of their lives.

After completing his first year in charge of the Jurisdiction of Asheville, and after a careful study of the manifold problems peculiar to it, Bishop Cheshire was convinced that the erection of the missionary jurisdiction was "an act of wise and prudent statesmanship." He thought that a missionary who had the oversight of three or four counties sorely needed regular visitations from the bishop, and in his opinion the work could be more effectively carried on if the bishop were able to remain a week or more with each missionary. He pressed these points upon the members of the House of Bishops in strongly advocating the election of a bishop for the Jurisdiction. Finally, in the fall of 1898, the House of Bishops elected the Rev. Junius Moore Horner, a native North Carolinian, as missionary bishop of the Jurisdiction of Asheville. He was consecrated on December 28, 1898, in Trinity Church, Asheville, with Bishop Cheshire as the consecrator. After this service Bishop Cheshire formally turned over to Bishop Horner the full administration of the Jurisdiction.

Turning now to a wholly different phase of Bishop Cheshire's work, we take up one of the most important achievements of his long episcopate, the establishment of St. Mary's School for girls as a church institution. This school had been founded in Raleigh by Dr. Aldert Smedes in 1842, and had been nurtured and maintained, through good and hard times, by its founder and his son and successor, Dr. Bennett Smedes. St. Mary's was not a church school, but its two rectors had been Episcopal clergymen, and thus the institution had been under the exclusive influence of the Episcopal Church. By 1896 Dr. Bennett Smedes was finding it very difficult to compete with publicly supported and privately endowed schools. At this time he made it known that he could no longer continue St. Mary's as a private school.

The Alumnae Association of St. Mary's at once took action to preserve the school for the church. It sent a memorial to the diocesan convention of 1896, in which it appealed to the Episcopal Church in North Carolina "either to endow the School, or to erect for it suitable buildings in Raleigh or elsewhere, and thus relieve it of one great drain, its heavy rent." The appeal met with sympathetic attention from Bishop Cheshire. Only the year before, he had remarked to the convention: "I have been, from earliest childhood, brought up to look upon St. Mary's School, at Raleigh, as the most valuable of all our church institutions or agencies in North Carolina. . . . I cannot too highly recommend this school to the confidence of all the people of North Carolina."

After careful consideration of the St. Mary's Alumnae memorial, the convention adopted a resolution providing for the appointment of a committee of six, to include the Bishop, with the authority to buy suitable buildings for a girls' school or to purchase land and erect new buildings. In direct reply to the memorialists, Bishop Cheshire offered a resolution, which the convention adopted, assuring the alumnae that the church in North Carolina "will do all in its power to place St. Mary's School upon a permanent foundation as an institution under the charge and patronage of the Church throughout the entire State. . . ."

At the convention of 1897 the special committee on a diocesan school for girls reported that it had procured a

First Years in the Episcopacy 65

charter of incorporation for the Board of Trustees of St. Mary's School from the state legislature, and had turned over to this corporation all further negotiations. The newly constituted Board of Trustees, of which Bishop Cheshire was chairman, then made its report. It recommended that not less than one hundred thousand dollars be raised for the purchase of a location, the erection of buildings, and an endowment of St. Mary's School. The Board announced that it had contracted to purchase for fifty thousand dollars a site known as the St. Mary's Tract. The convention adopted the report as it was made.

During the past year, at the request of the Trustees, Bishop Cheshire had spent a month visiting many towns throughout the state in an attempt to interest the people of the church in the needs and potentialities of St. Mary's School. His efforts met with gratifying success. He appealed to the women of the state, and especially to the alumnae of St. Mary's, to raise fifty thousand dollars for an endowment which should be known as "The St. Mary's Alumnae Association Fund." To stimulate the interest and increase the activity of the women in this plan, Bishop Cheshire organized the "Order of the Patrons and Daughters of St. Mary's." He proposed to find fifty women who would give five hundred dollars each towards the endowment, and two hundred and fifty others who would each contribute one hundred dollars. He reported to the convention of 1897 that he had raised a substantial amount in this way.

Thus, St. Mary's was established as the official school of the Episcopal Church in North Carolina. The Diocese of East Carolina and the Jurisdiction of Asheville had agreed to contribute to the maintenance of the school and were given representation on the Board of Trustees.

Dr. Bennett Smedes was retained as rector of the school and continued in this position until his death in 1899. The first year the school was under the control of the church the number of boarding students increased fifty per cent. To a great extent the enlarged enrollment was due to the renewed interest which Bishop Cheshire had aroused.

In the course of his negotiations to establish St. Mary's as a church school, the Bishop discovered that the churchmen of South Carolina had been for some time loyal and generous supporters of the school. After reflection upon this fact, he determined to ask the Diocese of South Carolina to co-operate in the maintenance and management of St. Mary's. When he discussed the subject with the Board of Trustees, it was decided to appoint a committee of the Board to meet at Saluda to confer with representatives from South Carolina. The conference was held in August, 1898. After a friendly and constructive discussion, the conference resolved that St. Mary's School should be placed under the "control and patronage of all the Carolina Dioceses."

Bishop Cheshire met with the convention of the Diocese of South Carolina in the spring of 1899 and presented the advantages and possibilities of St. Mary's as a church institution. The resolution of the Saluda conference was reported to the convention and was unanimously adopted. Bishop Capers, two clergymen, and two laymen were appointed to the Board of Trustees to represent South Carolina. After patient and diligent work Bishop Cheshire was able to unite the church of the two states in the support of one church school for girls. In a comparatively short time it was to become the largest Episcopal school for girls in the United States.

First Years in the Episcopacy

In the winter of 1897 Bishop Cheshire suffered an irreparable loss in the death of his wife. Their married life of twenty-two years had been remarkably happy. Mrs. Cheshire had been a great help to him in his work as deacon and priest and later as bishop of the Diocese. She gave him encouragement, devotion, and the benefit of her sound common sense. The Bishop often spoke of how much she meant to him in his work, and of their happy life together.

It was a fortunate coincidence that the Lambeth Conference came in the summer of 1897, for it enabled him to have a complete change, removing him from those associations which reminded him so strongly of his wife. The Lambeth Conference, which convenes approximately every ten years at Lambeth Palace, London, is composed of all the bishops of the Episcopal Church throughout the world. Bishop Cheshire decided to attend, believing it would be broadening and an exceedingly worth-while experience. The object of the Conference was to discuss religious questions of world-wide interest. In the course of its sessions it would be divided into groups which would discuss problems relating to particular countries.

The Bishop sailed from New York on June 2, arriving in England six days later. Since the Conference did not commence until July 1, he spent the intervening time sight-seeing. This was the summer of Queen Victoria's Diamond Jubilee, giving an additional interest to his trip. He attended the Jubilee service at St. Paul's, and remarked that the Bishop of London preached "a good sermon" for the occasion.

The Lambeth Conference was formally opened at Westminster Abbey by the Archbishop of Canterbury, who was to preside over its sessions. There were present for the Conference one hundred and ninety-four bishops from all parts of the world. Forty-nine of these represented the Episcopal Church of the United States. The sessions of the Conference continued through July 31. Bishop Cheshire was a member of the committee on church unity, and, as far as his journal reveals, this was the only committee on which he served. Reporting upon the Lambeth Conference to his diocesan convention the following year, Bishop Cheshire said: "The first message which we bring home from the Lambeth Conference of 1897 is that God in His Providence is opening the world to us; and to prepare us for the work we are to do, He is drawing all parts of the world-possessing Anglo-Saxon race into a closer union of common interest and sympathies, and of mutual confidence." He declared that the American bishops, while receiving much benefit from the Conference, had also contributed constructively to its work.

Shortly after the Conference closed, Bishop Cheshire visited the Archbishop of York for a few days. Upon leaving York he spent about a month traveling in England, Scotland, the Orkneys, and Ireland. In early September he left England for the Continent, where he visited in succession Antwerp, Brussels, and Cologne. Of his reactions to the cathedrals of these three cities, the Bishop observed that they "do not seem to me to be really so full of interest and beauty as even the inferior English cathedrals. They do not so abound with evidences and symbols of their connection with the life and history of the country and people, and so in spite of all their ornamentation they have a barren look." [8] The Bishop did some further sight-seeing in Germany, Switzerland, and France. While in Switzerland he saw the famous Lion of Lucerne, which he thought possessed "a dignity, noble-

First Years in the Episcopacy 69

ness, and beauty about it which exceeds anything of the kind I have ever seen before." Leaving from Southampton, he arrived in New York on September 24, feeling much refreshed and ready to return to the work of his Diocese.

Two years after his visit to England Bishop Cheshire married Miss Elizabeth Lansdale Mitchell, of Beltsville, Maryland. She was the daughter of Rev. Walter A. Mitchell, an Episcopal clergyman. The marriage proved to be happy and successful in every way. Mrs. Cheshire was a splendid mother to the Bishop's children, and they all became devoted to her.

When a friend heard that Bishop Cheshire was to be married, he remarked to the Bishop that with his large family he needed a wife. With his characteristic honesty the Bishop replied: "I don't need any such thing. My daughters take the best care of me and want me to have the best of everything. I don't need a wife; I am marrying again just because I want to." [9]

From the General Convention of 1895 to that of 1931, Bishop Cheshire attended every triennial meeting of this body. In the first three or four conventions, he did not take an active part in the discussions of the House of Bishops. For that matter, he never participated as prominently in its deliberations as some of the other bishops. At the 1895 convention he was appointed to the committees on the Admission of New Dioceses and on the Consecration of Bishops, and at the next triennial meeting he was made a member of the Joint Commission on the Revision of the Constitution and Canons. This last appointment pleased him, since it was the kind of work for which he was well prepared. His legal training influenced his partiality for this type of work. In 1904 he was appointed to the Committee on Canons, on which he served for almost every convention until his death. As a member of this committee he made his most important contribution to the work of the General Convention. It will be recalled that it was in this capacity that he had done his best work in the diocesan conventions. From time to time he was made a member of other regular and special committees.

When Bishop Cheshire assumed the office of bishop of the Diocese of North Carolina, he felt it his duty to exercise the full authority of that office. In deciding upon this course of action he did not intend to be arbitrary or despotic in administering the Diocese, although at times some clergymen and laymen seemed to think so. But when they became better acquainted with him and his methods, they admired and respected him the more. The Bishop had a forthright, and sometimes decidedly blunt, manner of speaking, which, to those who did not know him so well, seemed arbitrary or overbearing. He had disagreements with his clergymen, but they felt that they could always count upon receiving a fair hearing from him. When the Bishop realized he was in error upon any point, no one was quicker than he to admit it.

In 1895 Bishop Cheshire, for the first time in the history of the Diocese, issued to the clergy "Visitation Articles," as called for by a canon of the church. After employing them for a year he found they were useful and "calculated to make the visitations of the Bishop of more real value to the Clergy and to the people. The Bishop has for so long a time ceased to exert any real influence or control in the ordinary life and work of the parish in all parts of the United States, that the assertion of that authority, which in theory our Bishops are supposed to pos-

First Years in the Episcopacy

sess, is perhaps impracticable at present." [10] He thought that if the bishop would make himself acquainted with the affairs of each congregation during his visitation, it would strengthen the influence of the episcopate, and would go far towards the "breaking up of our present congregational parochialism." One of Bishop Cheshire's customs which endeared him to his people was that of calling upon the members of a congregation during his visitation. Of this practice he once remarked: "People like the attention and it makes Bishop and people feel nearer together, but in most cases they do not want very long visits." [11] The Bishop's keen understanding of human nature was one of his most notable qualities.

Bishop Cheshire thought that southern bishops had a great deal to be thankful for, particularly that in the South "as much as anywhere in the world, I believe, the Bishop may still be in some real and personal sense, the pastor of his flock, can live in familiar and confidential relations with his people." He deplored the tendency, which seemed to be growing in some quarters, of making the bishop simply an administrator of ecclesiastical affairs.

While Bishop Cheshire was in no sense a ritualist, or what is commonly known as high church, he believed in a strict adherence to the rubrics of the Book of Common Prayer. He had a great reverence and admiration for the services of the Prayer Book, and consequently little patience with those clergymen who attempted to alter their order or length. He was not a dogmatic formalist, but was thoroughly convinced that the canons and rubrics of the church should be obeyed and not disregarded by those individuals who might take exception to them.

In a charge to his clergy on the subject of Public Worship, Bishop Cheshire pointed out that the church was established and is sustained by Christ for two purposes: "first, to be the depository and source of spiritual Truth and Power; and second, to bring men into living contact with that spiritual Truth and Power." The Prayer Book is a means by which the church can diffuse and extend the truth, and it is also a means of developing and conserving the influence of the church. In his opinion, extemporary methods of worship had a tendency to weaken and finally destroy the concept of common public worship. The public worship of the Episcopal Church was not left to individual whim or judgment, but was definitely prescribed. He maintained that the participation of the congregation in the services and sacraments of the church is its principal means of cultivating its oneness with Christ. The Bishop enjoined the clergy to follow the services as they were set down in the Prayer Book, and warned them that they would gain nothing, but rather would injure the church by seeking to make their services more attractive through short cuts or innovations.

In a Pastoral Letter to the clergy and laity of the Diocese, Bishop Cheshire further developed the subject of public worship and the use of the Prayer Book. He gave much sound instruction as to how the minister and congregation should conduct themselves in any of the church's services, particularly emphasizing the importance of correct kneeling and audible and intelligent responses. He stressed the value which the clergy and laity would receive from a regular observance of the feast days and fast days. The Bishop expressed his strong disapproval of decorating the church for any purpose other than "for God's honor." The sacred character of the church should not be sacrificed to gratify the vanity of

First Years in the Episcopacy

men and women. He referred particularly to the extravagant excesses often indulged in when decorating the church for weddings.

This Pastoral Letter is just as applicable to churchmen today and is worthy of as much consideration from them as when it was first issued in 1912. It would be of great value to them to hear it read annually in the churches of the Diocese.

Bishop Cheshire never went to extremes in anything. In spiritual as well as in material matters he believed in preserving a sense of proportion. He advised his clergy to use practical judgment in the observance of Lenten services. Very few clergymen were capable of preaching good sermons for forty or more consecutive days and, in his opinion, few congregations desired them. Even in those cases where a preaching Lent had been successful, he thought that a change would have a salutary effect upon the people.

On the subject of church music he tried to preserve an equilibrium of opinion. The Bishop was very fond of good ecclesiastical music and thoroughly enjoyed singing himself. While his standards of church music were high, he did not at all approve of too elaborate arrangements of the old chants and hymns. He wanted them sung properly, but also in such a way that at least a part of the congregation would be able to join in with the choir. On several occasions he was known to have stopped the organist and choir in the middle of a hymn or chant because the tune was either too difficult or too decorative.

Bishop Cheshire's interest in domestic missionary work was by no means limited to the zeal which he had displayed when working in the mountains of North Carolina. In his report on missionary work to the convention of 1898, he made a strong appeal for domestic missions and missionaries. He called to the attention of the convention the fact that the growth of the church in the Diocese was chiefly through its missions. Since there were no large city parishes, its strength lay in the towns, villages, and country districts. "In these," said he, "has been our growth, and in these is our hope and strength for the future." The missionary clergymen had presented for confirmation during the past year more than half of the total number of persons confirmed. He concluded these remarks with an urgent plea for adequate salaries for the missionaries.

Up to 1901 the administration of the diocesan missions was in the hands of the Bishop and the Executive Missionary Committee of the convention. Bishop Cheshire reported that under this system the missionary work usually showed an annual deficit of from four to five hundred dollars, even after he had used funds for it which should have been reserved for special work. With the advice and approbation of Bishop Cheshire, the convention of 1901 divided the missionary work of the Diocese into three divisions—the Convocation of Raleigh, the Convocation of Charlotte, and the Convocation for Colored Work. These convocations, each with an archdeacon at its head, were given full control of diocesan missions. The archdeacons, under the supervision of the bishop, had the direction and control of the missionaries in their respective convocations. Under this new organization the diocesan missions progressed steadily, and the treasurers of the convocations seldom reported a deficit. Some fifteen years after this plan was inaugurated, Bishop Cheshire declared that the missionary work had been

First Years in the Episcopacy 75

"prosecuted with greater vigor and system than ever before in my knowledge of the Diocese."

At the close of the first decade of Bishop Cheshire's episcopate, a large number of clergy and laity gathered at Good Shepherd Church, Raleigh, on the evening of October 14, 1903, to celebrate the occasion. At this service the Bishop made an address in which he reviewed his work for the period. During the decade he had held more than 4,000 services, preached 1,400 sermons, delivered 500 addresses, confirmed 4,400 persons, consecrated 27 churches and chapels, and ordained 27 clergymen. To him the greatest achievement of the past ten years was the acquisition of St. Mary's and its establishment as the church school of all the Carolina dioceses. In 1897 his Diocese had assumed in behalf of St. Mary's an obligation of fifty thousand dollars to be paid in twenty years. At the end of six years only eighteen thousand dollars of the debt remained, and in addition ten thousand dollars had been spent upon permanent equipment for the school. Since the Diocese took over St. Mary's, the number of boarding pupils had increased threefold. In conclusion, he declared that they should not look too much to the past but should press on to the future with the work of the church.

Representatives of the clergy and laity congratulated the Bishop upon his tenth anniversary, pledging their loyalty and devotion to him, and expressing the appreciation of their respective bodies for his splendid work. Mr. Richard H. Battle, in behalf of a number of the Bishop's friends, presented him with a beautiful pectoral cross and a silk cassock. In acknowledging the kind expressions and gifts, the Bishop remarked: "I have one single desire, it is to serve God in this Diocese. It was the interest that I took in the work here that brought me into the ministry, and I have no desire to labor elsewhere. I love my people, and I appreciate the kindness, sympathy and aid that has been given me...."[12]

The following day the colored clergy and laity honored the Bishop in a service at St. Ambrose Church, Raleigh. Resolutions expressing the confidence and affection of the colored churchmen were presented to Bishop Cheshire by Rev. Henry B. Delany. Rev. Primus P. Alston, on behalf of the colored clergy, gave the Bishop a handsome stole, accompanying it with an address expressing the gratitude of the colored people for his work among them. Afterwards, the Bishop observed that nothing during the past ten years had been more gratifying to him than "the unvarying respect, courtesy and loyal support" which he had received at the hands of his colored clergy and laity.

CHAPTER VI

Man and Bishop

In addition to his accomplishments as a clergyman, prelate, and scholar, Bishop Cheshire attained considerable skill and reputation as a sportsman. Fishing and hunting were the sports he liked best and the only ones he indulged in. He once remarked that he had been fond of fishing from his boyhood, but he thought his liking for it increased with age. His prowess as a fisherman was well known to his churchmen from the coast to the mountains of North Carolina. During the 1890's, when he was building up his mountain work, he would sometimes allow himself a few hours of relaxation to fish for the fine trout in the cold mountain streams. As a good fisherman should, he always carried his tackle with him when traveling near promising streams. In later years, whenever he had the opportunity, he returned to the mountains for a brief vacation of fishing.

On one of these trips, accompanied by his son, Joseph B. Cheshire, Jr., he was fishing in the Watauga River. When they came to a ford, the Bishop recalled that he had an old friend, Bill Holler, living a short distance away, whom he would like very much to see. Accordingly, they walked up the road about a half mile. Pausing at the foot of a mountainside, the Bishop asked his son to climb up and tell Mr. Holler that an old friend wanted to see him, but not to mention his name. Shortly afterwards, his son returned accompanied by a little old man, with long white hair and beard and a pleasant, wrinkled face. As soon as the old man saw his visitor, his face lit up with a smile, he threw open his arms, rushed up to the Bishop, and embraced him, crying: "Lord! It's the old Bishop, the old Bishop, the old Bishop!"

The Bishop's fondness for hunting was almost as great as that for fishing. He began hunting in early boyhood but, according to his own statement, he never became a good shot. Many of his hunting companions, however, would undoubtedly contest the point. Among the people of his Diocese he was famous for his skill in wild turkey hunting. Strange as it may seem, he did not kill a wild turkey until he was sixty-four years old. Up to that time he had hunted partridges a great deal, but as he grew older, he had to give it up because it required so much walking. Hunting wild turkeys, although strenuous enough, was better suited to his years. After his first kill, scarcely a season passed that he did not bag at least one turkey. As the Bishop's enthusiasm for this sport grew, he made an interesting collection of turkey calls. They ranged from several varieties made from the wing bone of the turkey to the box type, which was usually made of cedar.

Less than a month before his death Bishop Cheshire went turkey hunting in the Roanoke River swamp, near Scotland Neck. On this occasion, at the age of eighty-two, he killed a fine gobbler. About a week later he was to go to St. Stephen's Church, Oxford, for a visitation

Bishop Cheshire fishing in the French Broad River, September, 1912.

Photograph by Bayard Wootten

The Parker-Cheshire House in Tarboro, birthplace of Bishop Cheshire. The house was built by Theophilus Parker, the Bishop's grandfather.

Man and Bishop

and planned while there to go turkey shooting with his friend, Rev. Reuben Meredith, rector of the church. His son Godfrey was to join them for the hunt on Monday. A few days before leaving home, however, he did not feel at all well and, after consulting his physician, informed his daughter, Miss Sarah Cheshire, he would give up the hunt. But by Saturday the Bishop was feeling so much better that on his way to Oxford he wrote his daughter the following letter:

"Dear Sarah:

When Godfrey comes to Oxford tomorrow have him bring my gun and the bag in which I keep my hunting clothes and turkey calls. I am going turkey hunting on Monday.

'When the devil was sick the devil a monk would be,
When the devil was well the devil a monk was he.'

      Your affectionate father,
      Joseph Blount Cheshire"

Bishop Cheshire had an enviable reputation throughout the state as a raconteur of rare charm. Some of his best stories came from his fishing and hunting experiences, but they covered many other subjects as well. Most of his best anecdotes of personalities and events in North Carolina history are found in his book *Nonnulla*. It was not always the content of his stories which caught and held the interest of his listeners, but quite as often the manner in which the Bishop told them. For this reason they sometimes lose their color and charm when read or repeated by someone else. When he told an amusing story, which he often did, one of its best features was his own enjoyment in the telling and his hearty, contagious laughter. Another characteristic of the Bishop's stories was the natural way they appeared in his conversation, usually graphically illustrating or emphasizing a point. He never dragged a story into his conversation merely for the pleasure of telling it.

As a conversationalist, however, he did not depend upon his ability to tell a good story. He could talk interestingly to persons from any walk of life, seeming always to know just the right thing to say to each. He never flattered, but gave freely his candid opinion whenever requested. Although he talked a great deal himself, the Bishop made his listener feel that he was interested in his ideas and wanted to hear them.

In his role as a preacher of sermons Bishop Cheshire did not resemble his modern prototype, who quite often is more of a brilliant lecturer than a preacher. The Bishop employed no oratory in his sermons, but preached very much as if he were talking to a group of friends. He took a text from the Bible, most frequently from the New Testament, and proceeded to expound and interpret it, seldom using stories or anecdotes to illustrate his ideas. They were unadorned, straightforward expositions of religious truth. Of his sermons, the Bishop remarked to one of his clergymen, "Because a man is not converted to Christ through my teaching and preaching, I do not on that account conclude that he has rejected Christ; he has only rejected my representation of Christ."

Dr. Robert B. Drane, for more than fifty years rector of St. Paul's Church, Edenton, once wrote of a rather typical reaction to the Bishop's sermons. He invited a man, who scarcely ever came to church, to come to St. Paul's to hear Bishop Cheshire. The man said he would be glad to, that he had heard the Bishop preach several times, and that he "always talked sense." Dr. Drane remarked that if the thousands of persons who belonged to no church could be made to realize that "preachers did really talk sense," the membership of the churches would increase and religion would be more respected.

While not meaning to belittle the value of sermons, Bishop Cheshire sincerely felt that the prayers, responses, chants, and hymns of the church's service, climaxed by the supreme act of Christian worship, the celebration of the Holy Communion, held a greater significance for mankind and better satisfied spiritual needs.

Bishop Cheshire's interest and activities extended to all phases of the church's life in his Diocese. There was scarcely any work or endeavor of his people too small to attract his attention. He often remarked that it is "the little things that count." It was his capacity to understand and sympathize with the everyday problems of his people that so greatly endeared him to them. Although the Bishop never in any way permitted himself or his clergy to become involved in controversial political affairs, he displayed at all times a vital interest in the social problems of his state. When he felt it to be the duty of the church to take a positive stand on a social question, he did not hesitate to make clear her position and to take what action he believed best suited to the occasion.

The increasing number of divorces in North Carolina and the growing laxity of the laws on that subject was a problem which gave the Bishop much concern. In 1904 he called the matter to the attention of his diocesan convention and suggested a remedy for the situation.

The Bishop asserted that there had been sufficient talk and theorizing upon the divorce question and that now was the time for positive action. The apathy of the public conscience, which had permitted the divorce law to be greatly modified, was, in his opinion, the cause of the divorce evil. Bishop Cheshire believed there was only one true reason for divorce: adultery. For many years it had been the only cause recognized by the state law, but in recent years frequent changes in the law to meet individual cases had created an unjustifiable condition. Not one of these modifications of the law had been adopted upon "any general principle of morals or of social science."

The Bishop called upon the convention to express its condemnation of the present legislation on the divorce question, and to issue an address to the people of the state urging the necessity of reforming the divorce laws. He also suggested that the convention appoint a committee to communicate with the other Christian bodies of the state in order to secure united action on the subject. After serious deliberation, the convention indorsed the Bishop's position. It authorized him to appoint a committee, of which he should be chairman, to publish an address to the people of the state expressing the sentiment of the Episcopal Church on the divorce question; and to prepare a memorial to the General Assembly requesting that the divorce laws be restored to the status of the code of 1883. The convention sent a request to the Diocese of East Carolina, the Jurisdiction of Asheville, and all the other denominations of the state to join in this memorial.

Bishop Cheshire lost no time in forwarding to every church conference or synod, meeting prior to January,

1905, the resolutions of his diocesan convention. Favorable action was taken on the resolutions by the Presbyterian, Methodist, Baptist, and Methodist Protestant churches. The Bishop attended the Presbyterian Synod and the Conference of the Methodist Church, and was cordially received.

When the General Assembly met in 1905, Governor Robert B. Glenn recommended that the divorce laws be restored to the form as found in the code of 1883. After a close consideration of the memorial of the North Carolina churches, the legislature enacted a law which embodied in substance the request of the memorialists.

Bishop Cheshire once more concerned himself with the divorce problem when the legislature of 1931 was considering several bills for modifying the conditions for granting divorces. At the time the bills were under discussion he was visiting his daughter in Louisiana. In order to place his views on the subject before the legislature, the Bishop addressed a letter to the chairman of the Judiciary Committee of the House of Representatives. It was published in the *News and Observer* of February 12.

He again attacked the practice of enacting special laws for particular persons, and asserted that in some incidents the laws were unconstitutional. He reviewed the efforts which he and many other citizens had made about twenty-five years before to restrict the causes for granting divorce. With public opinion behind them, their efforts had been successful, but since that time many of the old abuses had reappeared. The Bishop declared that from his knowledge of public opinion in North Carolina, sentiment against relaxing the divorce laws was as strong then as it had been twenty-five years before. In his letter he confined himself to one principal idea, "the will of the people of the State against personal influence in behalf of individual parties," believing that it would produce a greater effect than if he merely reiterated the usual moral and social arguments.

It cannot be said with certainty how much effect the Bishop's letter had on the members of the legislature, but coming from a man whose character and opinions were held in such high regard by North Carolinians, it must have had some influence upon the outcome. The proposed measures were defeated by large majorities in the General Assembly.

On one of the most controversial questions of the twentieth century, national prohibition, Bishop Cheshire held very definite views. He believed that each state should be allowed to decide the question for itself, and that a federal prohibition law would breed more evil than good.

Several years before the passage of the national prohibition law, Bishop Cheshire attended a meeting in Raleigh which was considering various aspects of social welfare work. He was present as an invited guest. The business of the meeting was moving along smoothly, when someone introduced a resolution to the effect that the meeting should memorialize Congress with a demand that the manufacture and sale of alcoholic beverages be made illegal in the United States. The resolution was received with much enthusiasm. Many speeches were made advocating its passage and all were applauded. After the enthusiasm had somewhat subsided and the question was about to be put, Bishop Cheshire asked permission to say a few words. He stated that he deplored excessive drinking and its evil consequences, suffered as much if not more by the innocent as well as the drinker. He sympathized with the purpose of the resolution to achieve more widespread temperance, but, he reminded them, good intentions unless intelligently directed often did more harm than good. Under the American system each state or community had the authority to outlaw liquor, as had already been done in North Carolina. So long as the prohibition of liquor was confined to those states whose public opinion was behind it, he believed it could be enforced. He did not think, however, that a federal law could be enforced in those states where public opinion and the state authorities were in opposition. He maintained that what had already been accomplished in some states in behalf of temperance would be jeopardized if an attempt was made to impose prohibition upon those states which were not yet ready for it.

Upon the conclusion of the Bishop's remarks, there was for a few moments complete silence. It was as if someone had thrown cold water over the entire meeting. When a member moved that the resolution be laid on the table, not a voice was raised in opposition to the motion, and the subject was dropped. The Bishop was never one to allow his intelligence to be overruled by emotionalism, and in stating his views on national prohibition he not only displayed his sound judgment but also proved himself a very good prophet.

Bishop Cheshire exercised a remarkable influence upon the people of his Diocese. One aspect of the effect of his character upon them is seen in the ready co-operation and assistance they gave him in his work for the church. The inspiration they caught from him was not a transient enthusiasm, but one which carried over from one endeavor to another. Above all, the Episcopalians of the Diocese loved their Bishop as a man—a vital, interesting personality who possessed none of the unctuous pompousness of the commonplace ecclesiastic. Miss Nell Battle Lewis once aptly characterized the Bishop as "much more than a Churchman, able Churchman though he is. Foremost, he is a man—a gentleman—of the most unswerving honesty, conviction, courage, kindness, humor, and charm." [1]

Throughout almost all of his Episcopate Bishop Cheshire had no secretary. By choice he attended to his correspondence himself, writing all of his letters in longhand. Towards the end of his life he employed a secretary for a short time, but soon found that he preferred to do the work himself. He kept letter-books in which he entered a record of every letter he wrote, giving the name of the person written to, the date, and the place he was writing from. According to his own records, he wrote during his Episcopate 66,778 letters. The Bishop never liked any help in doing something which he felt he was able to do for himself.

As a father Bishop Cheshire won the admiration of everyone who knew him. Each of his three daughters and three sons gave him their wholehearted love, obedience, and respect throughout his lifetime. He gained and held their devotion by his kindness, intelligence, and sympathetic understanding. He was a strict disciplinarian, but always preserved a tolerant and open-minded attitude towards the desires and weaknesses of youth. He treated his sons as men and expected them to act the part.

The Bishop gave his children all the advantages he could afford. Two of his sons were educated at the

University of North Carolina, and the third attended the University of the South. His three daughters all went to St. Mary's School. When one of his sons was leaving home to enter college, the Bishop told him that he would not ask him to promise to refrain from forming bad habits at school, such as drinking and gambling, nor would he accept such a promise if his son offered it. He went on to say that he had tried to teach him right from wrong and that his son well knew what things he could do that would make his father happy and proud and those which would make him unhappy and ashamed. He wanted his son to conduct himself as a gentleman, not because of any promises made, but for the sake of decency. The Bishop asked him to remember that he would always stand up for him as long as he was in the right, but he would not defend him for a moment if he were ever guilty of misconduct. This straightforward, manly counsel made a lasting impression upon the son. It was typical of the Bishop's uncompromising and practical way of thinking on moral questions.

CHAPTER VII

Historian

From his youth Bishop Cheshire had been fond of history, and as he grew older, his interest in it developed into a serious avocation. While practicing law in Tarboro, he saw a good deal of his uncle-in-law, ex-Governor Henry Clark, who had a decided taste for history. He had an excellent library to which he made his nephew welcome. Cheshire spent many happy hours browsing among the old books and manuscripts and listening to the conversation of his uncle. Governor Clark had a thorough acquaintance with the early history of North Carolina, particularly that of his own section. In later years Bishop Cheshire said of his uncle: "I have often felt that he had a greater influence than any other person in developing my tastes and inclinations in the direction of historical inquiry." [1]

For his first serious historical composition Cheshire chose a subject with which he was intimately acquainted, the history of the church in Edgecombe County. In a series of articles, under the title, "An Historical Sketch of the Church in Edgecombe County, North Carolina," which appeared in the *Church Messenger* from August

17 through September 21, 1880, he traced the history of this parish from the colonial period through the rectorate of his father. The sketch is superior to the usual parish history in that it concerned itself with the growth and development of the church in Edgecombe rather than with the genealogy of the families in that county.

When Colonel William L. Saunders was in the process of compiling the *Colonial Records of North Carolina*, he asked Cheshire to make a collection of documents relating to the colonial Episcopal Church. Cheshire secured from Bishop Perry of Iowa, Historiographer of the Episcopal Church, a large body of material, which he had copied under his personal supervision. Colonel Saunders found the material so interesting and valuable that he incorporated it in its entirety in the several volumes of the *Colonial Records*. In appreciation of his contribution Cheshire was given a full set of this work. In 1893 Judge Walter Clark, when he began to edit the *State Records of North Carolina*, wrote Bishop Cheshire: "I beg that you will aid me with your advice, suggestions and information as to what should be published and the best means of procuring materials." [2] This statement well illustrates the high regard in which the Bishop's historical acumen was generally held.

In 1883, in the course of collecting materials for Colonel Saunders, Cheshire visited Philadelphia. While there he examined the records of the Pennsylvania Quakers for information concerning the early Quaker settlements in North Carolina. From his examination of these records he found sufficient evidence to disprove the long-held thesis that the early settlers of North Carolina were religious refugees from New England and Virginia. His conclusion was that the first settlers of the Albemarle section came there primarily for economic reasons and not for religious freedom. He embodied his findings in a pamphlet called "The First Settlers of North Carolina Not Religious Refugees." After reading the monograph, Colonel Saunders wrote Cheshire: "You have not only *proved your proposition; You have demonstrated it.*" [3] Saunders adopted the same interpretation in his preface to the first volume of the *Colonial Records*. Cheshire's original thesis was further expanded and substantiated by future historians of the state.

In 1882 Cheshire edited and published the documents relating to the four conventions, held between 1790 and 1794, which had made the abortive attempt to set up a diocesan organization in North Carolina. The documents of three of these conventions had never been published before. They threw much light upon an important phase of the early history of the Episcopal Church in North Carolina.

The Diocese recognized Cheshire's ability as an historian by electing him historiographer at the convention of 1884. The convention of 1876 had created this office, and had elected Dr. M. M. Marshall, Rector of Christ Church, Raleigh, the first historiographer. It had also passed a resolution requiring each clergyman to compile a history of his parish. When Cheshire became historiographer eight years later, only a few of the clergy had complied with the resolution. After examining the histories which had been written, he found that, with a few exceptions, they were of no value. Several months after his election, in an article for the *Church Messenger*, he stressed the importance of preserving local church history. He announced that he was making a collection of old documents and pamphlets on church history for the

Historian

Diocese, and he requested anyone possessing these materials to send them to him. One of Cheshire's chief contributions as historiographer was the interest he aroused among the churchmen in the history of the church and of their respective parishes.

The publication of the *Colonial Records of North Carolina* further stimulated his interest in historical research. He planned and began to write the "Annals of the Church in the Province of North Carolina." He worked upon this history whenever he found an opportunity, but after his election as bishop his duties were so pressing that he had to abandon the project. He had made considerable progress, however, before laying it aside. His research was not done in vain, for he was able to use much of it in one of the papers he presented before the centennial convention of the dioceses of East Carolina and North Carolina in 1890.

Probably Cheshire's most productive act as historiographer of the Diocese was to initiate and successfully direct the celebration of the one-hundredth anniversary of the convention of 1790. This convention, held in Tarboro, had made the first, although unsuccessful, attempt to form a diocese in North Carolina. As the centennial of the event drew near, Cheshire thought that it should be commemorated in some appropriate manner. Accordingly, at the diocesan convention of 1889 he introduced a series of resolutions calling for a joint convention of the dioceses of North Carolina and East Carolina to be held at Tarboro the following year. The resolutions were adopted and a committee on arrangements appointed, with Dr. Jarvis Buxton as chairman. Commenting on the proceedings, Cheshire frankly remarked: "I took care, however, to get myself elected Secretary of the Committee; and the Committee cheerfully allowed me to do all the work." [4]

The Committee on Arrangements decided that the most fitting and profitable manner of celebrating the occasion would be to present a series of papers on the history of the Episcopal Church in North Carolina. Cheshire organized the program, selecting the writers and the subjects of the papers.

The joint convention met in Tarboro May 16-18, 1890, and was well attended by churchmen from both dioceses. The papers covered the history of the church in the colony, its decay following the Revolution, and its revival after 1817. Cheshire read a paper on "The Church in the Province of North Carolina." At the close of the proceedings, the convention resolved that the addresses should be published in book form under Cheshire's editorial direction. Upon the motion of the Rev. Robert Strange, it was also resolved: "That the thanks of the joint Convention of North and East Carolina be extended to the Rev. J. B. Cheshire, Jr., for conceiving and carrying to so successful an issue the reunion which has been so delightful and edifying to us all."

Since there was not sufficient time, all of the addresses prepared for the joint convention were not delivered. In addition to the paper Cheshire read, he also wrote two others—"Decay and Revival, 1800-1830" and "White Haven Church and the Rev. Robert Johnston Miller." These papers, as well as all the others written for the centennial celebration, were published in a volume entitled *Sketches of Church History in North Carolina*. Besides the three papers and his editorial work, Cheshire wrote the introduction to this book. The vol-

Historian

ume is a distinct contribution to the history of the Episcopal Church in North Carolina. Prior to this time little of any value had been written on the subject. Cheshire's articles are probably more scholarly than any of the others, and they definitely reveal more research in original sources.

In recognition of Cheshire's achievements as a clergyman and his contributions as a historian, the University of North Carolina at its commencement of 1890 conferred upon him the degree of Doctor of Divinity. Four years later the University of the South bestowed upon him the same honor, and in 1916 his alma mater, Trinity College, Hartford, Connecticut, also gave him the degree of Doctor of Divinity. He was not one to seek honors, but when they were conferred upon him he appreciated them, particularly the thought which motivated the bestowal. Bishop Cheshire became an honorary member of the North Carolina Society of the Cincinnati in 1897 and a few years later an hereditary member. He served for a time as chaplain of the North Carolina Society and later of the national organization.

Although his diocesan work occupied most of his time, the Bishop found the opportunity now and again throughout his episcopate to write articles for ecclesiastical and historical publications. The subject matter of most of his writings was drawn chiefly from North Carolina history. One of his most interesting departures from this practice was the editing of George Herbert's *A Priest to the Temple or, the Country Parson, His Character and Rule of Holy Life*. This work, first published in 1652, had attracted his attention when he was a young lawyer in Baltimore. He was greatly impressed at the time with its earnestness and its spiritual character. When

94   Bishop Joseph Blount Cheshire

in 1905 Professor Palmer, of Harvard University, edited the complete works of Herbert, the *Country Parson* was again brought to the Bishop's attention. He decided to bring out a special edition of the *Country Parson* in order to make it available to all of the clergy. The work appeared in 1908 and was dedicated to his father, whose sixty years in the ministry splendidly illustrated Herbert's ideal of a country parson. In his introduction to the book Bishop Cheshire commented: "It is not too much to say of it that for beauty and truth to nature, for its combination of the ideal and the practical, for its presentation of an almost heavenly perfection in terms of human experience, it has not its equal in the religious literature of our language." Whenever sending out a young clergyman as a country parson, he always tried to supply him with a copy of this work, believing that it would be of great value to him and his parishioners.

At the request of the editor of the *Carolina Churchman* Bishop Cheshire wrote, in 1910–1911, a sketch of the life of each of his predecessors, Bishops Ravenscroft, Ives, Atkinson, and Lyman. He did not make the sketches serious biographical studies, but tried to present intimate pictures of the four bishops, including a few amusing anecdotes. The sketch of Bishop Ravenscroft is probably the best and the most interesting.

In the course of 1910 and 1911, at the invitation of the Episcopal seminaries at Sewanee, Alexandria, New York, Philadelphia, Cambridge, and Middletown, Bishop Cheshire delivered a series of lectures on the history of the Episcopal Church in the Confederate States. The lectures were well received, and upon their conclusion the Bishop was urged to put them in permanent form. Real-

Historian

izing that the interest in the subject was fairly widespread, he decided to arrange the lectures for publication. In 1912 Longmans, Green, and Company published them under the title, *The Church in the Confederate States.*

In this work the Bishop describes the organization of the Episcopal Church in the Confederacy, the church's work among the soldiers, its attitude towards the Negroes, its trials and burdens, its publications, and, finally, the reunion of the northern and southern branches of the church. Following the last chapter he included a brief study of the life of Thomas Atkinson, Bishop of North Carolina, 1853-1881, who had been one of the most important exponents of the reunion of the church in 1865.

In general, the critics praised the Bishop's work as a significant contribution. Of it the *Outlook* remarked: "His account of the attitude of the Church in its political relations throughout those sad and trying times is free from any tinge of bitterness. Its narrative of the work of bishops and councils, and of the ministries of the church to the soldiers and to the slaves, deserves to be widely read for the little-known facts it records." *The Churchman,* of New York, declared: "The temper of Bishop Cheshire's narrative is admirable, his account of perplexing constitutional questions that arose from the relations of the Church to the Confederacy and to the Union is clear, his analysis of the issues is penetrating and acute, his conclusions will be generally accepted." The church periodicals, North and South, were unanimous in their praise of the Bishop's work. They felt he had done the American Episcopal Church a great service in preserving this phase of her history. The *Church Times,* of London, thought that while the book was interesting and informative, it was not fair to the northern church. Many of the reviewers considered the last chapter of the work, which discussed the reunion of the church in 1865, the most interesting and significant. The Bishop was able to write of this particular subject with intimacy, since his father had taken an active part in the reunion.

The Church in the Confederate States is Bishop Cheshire's most important historical contribution. In it his style is direct, simple, and restrained. It describes and interprets a phase of Civil War history which had never before been adequately treated, and since its publication no work on the subject has superseded it. For his information Bishop Cheshire relied almost entirely upon original sources. Some of the more personal incidents, however, were gained from actual participants in that stormy period.

On one of his visitations to Milnor Jones' missions in Watauga County, Bishop Cheshire told Jones that if he should outlive him he would see that some recognition was made of Jones' work. Many years later the Bishop fulfilled his promise by writing the volume, *Milnor Jones, Deacon and Missionary*. The greater part of this biography is devoted to the years 1894–1897, which Jones spent in the mountains of North Carolina. It is an interesting picture of that most unique character, and a good description of both the difficult and sometimes amusing sides of missionary work in the mountains. Although the Bishop liked and admired Jones, he did not fail to bring out his faults as well as his many virtues.

Bishop Cheshire's last important literary work * was

---

* For a complete list of the Bishop's published writings, see pp. 131-133.

Historian

his reminiscences of personalities and incidents in North Carolina history. He gave these memories the title *Nonnulla*, meaning "Not Nothings." The Bishop began this book on his seventy-fifth birthday, and completed it five years later. He included in it stories and anecdotes about people and places not customarily found in the serious histories, but which are not entirely without significance "as illustrating, in an informal and familiar way, the life of our State and our people." *Nonnulla* is replete with human interest to North Carolinians, and contributes much to their understanding of some of the characters who helped to build their state.

In recognition of Bishop Cheshire's contributions to North Carolina history, the State Literary and Historical Association elected him its president for 1931. In his presidential address the Bishop discussed the religious provisions of the Fundamental Constitutions prepared by John Locke for the Lords Proprietors of Carolina. Although Locke's document was never put into effect, its provisions for religious freedom, in the Bishop's opinion, "perhaps found lodgment in the life of the people and attained a better development in their subsequent history."[5] While the Church of England was made the established church of the colony, liberty of conscience was permitted to all except atheists. Elaborating upon the theme of religious freedom, he demonstrated that the colonial government did not practice religious intolerance even though laws were enacted for the support of an established church.

With his presidential address to the State Literary and Historical Association, Bishop Cheshire concluded his work as an historian. It was a fitting close to this phase of his life. Although history had been to him a pleasant avocation, no professional historian ever took his work more seriously or had a higher ideal of historical accuracy. In the words of Dr. A. R. Newsome, of the University of North Carolina, "Native ability, industry and self-discipline enabled him to achieve a degree of historical scholarship seldom encountered among laymen." The Episcopal Church in North Carolina owes him a debt of lasting gratitude for his pioneer work in its history.

CHAPTER VIII

Work Among the Colored People

Bishop Cheshire's active interest in the church's work among the Negroes began when he was rector of St. Peter's Church, Charlotte. His organization of the colored mission of St. Michael and All Angels and the part he took in helping to establish the Good Samaritan Hospital have already been related. When he became bishop he continued and greatly enlarged his activities in behalf of the Negro work.

In the early part of his episcopate the Bishop made an address to the Conference of Church Workers Among Colored People, in which he expressed some interesting ideas on the colored work. He first pointed out that the reconstruction acts had failed to accomplish for the Negro many of their designed objectives. Although those acts were for the most part of a purely political character, he realized many sincere people in the North had advocated them in the belief that they would help the Negro. In his opinion, the legislation of the reconstruction period had not accomplished for the colored people what its sincerest advocates had confidently expected. If the Negroes are to play a significant role in the future of this country, the Bishop declared, "it will be only because they shall have become fitted for that part. No theories of predominant political equality will avail for preserving privileges which are not exercised for the benefit of the community...." He believed that the disabilities of the Negro could not be removed, nor the disadvantages under which he worked conquered, by legislation against particular evils, "but simply by changing the actual conditions of the race itself." Those who are interested in the welfare of the Negro must work for the elevation of his ideals of living, of working, and of self-restraint. The Bishop emphasized the importance of developing a spirit of self-reliance and self-help among the colored clergy and laity, believing this to be the best means by which they could strengthen their economic and social position.

The colored churchmen of the Diocese soon learned that in Bishop Cheshire they had a staunch friend and one from whom they could count upon receiving a fair and sympathetic hearing. He reciprocated this confidence with a like faith in them. It was a regular practice of the Bishop to attend only the first day's session of the annual meetings of the white and colored convocations. He did this in order to give the clergy an opportunity of "speaking their mind freely." He always remembered an observation of George Eliot that "the first thing the clergy do, when they get together in convocation, is to abuse the Bishop." In this connection Bishop Cheshire once remarked: "I do not know what the white clergy may do, but I do not believe my black clergy will have anything to say against me even in my absence." [1]

At the opening of the twentieth century one of the most important questions facing the Episcopal Church in

Work Among the Colored People

the South was the separation of the Negro work in each diocese from that of the white. Bishop Cheshire was strongly opposed to any separation of the church's work founded solely on the racial feeling. He disliked to see the unity of the Diocese disrupted, and believed the ideal situation was "a church and a diocese which in its annual gatherings should represent visibly the oneness of all races and colors in Christ." [2] He realized, however, that he could not be guided entirely by his personal feelings on a question of such importance. A large body of the Negro clergy and many white churchmen throughout the South felt that the welfare of the church demanded some sort of separate organization for the colored work.

When he met his diocesan convention in the spring of 1907, Bishop Cheshire announced his position on this question. Since the colored people seemed to desire an organization of their own, he believed the time had come for the church to take some definite action. He asked the convention to make known its views on the question of separation, since it would come up for discussion in the General Convention that fall. The Bishop stated that two plans of organization for the Negroes were being considered. One provided for the consecration of suffragan bishops who should have charge of the colored clergy and laity and should be under the diocesan bishop. The other called for the consecration of missionary bishops who should have charge of the colored work in contiguous dioceses and who should be responsible to the General Convention. The Bishop declared that he was heartily in favor of the latter plan, believing that it met the needs of existing conditions much more justly and adequately than the former. Moreover, the colored people themselves seemed to favor the plan of using missionary bishops. If they were used they would be under the direct control of the General Convention and would be given more independence than suffragan bishops, who would be under the administrative jurisdiction of the white diocesan bishop. Bishop Cheshire felt that if the colored work was to be made independent of the white, the Negro bishops should be given some administrative as well as spiritual responsibilities.

When the convention took up the question of the colored work, it referred the whole matter to a special committee. After careful study, the committee recommended that the Negroes be given a separate organization, that the plan of missionary bishops be adopted, and that the deputies from the Diocese should present these recommendations to the General Convention. The committee's report was adopted.

At the General Convention, which met in the fall of 1907, the Conference of Church Workers among Colored People presented a memorial in which it advocated a separate organization for the Negroes and the election of suffragan bishops. A joint committee of the House of Bishops and the House of Deputies, of which Bishop Cheshire was made a member, was appointed to consider the memorial. This committee recommended the adoption of the principal features of the memorial. Bishop Cheshire and one other member of the committee presented a minority report in which they urged the use of missionary bishops. Their report was defeated in the House of Bishops by a vote of fifty to thirty-four, while that of the majority was carried, forty-five to thirty-three. After the defeat of his proposal, Bishop Cheshire voted for the majority's report, believing it preferable to no action on the subject.

Work Among the Colored People 103

The question of the racial episcopate was, however, far from being settled. During the next three meetings of the General Convention Bishop Cheshire and a few others continued to work for the adoption of the plan of missionary bishops. In 1913 they succeeded in getting the plan approved by the House of Bishops, but it was defeated by the House of Deputies. The southern bishops and clergy were the most undecided as to what plan they wanted to put into effect. Up to 1918 the Diocese of North Carolina had taken no action towards electing a suffragan bishop for the colored work. In 1917 Bishop Cheshire advised his diocesan convention to consider the question. The next year the convention voted to proceed to the election of a suffragan bishop.

Before nominations for the office were called for, Bishop Cheshire gathered together the colored clergy and laity of the convention for an informal discussion. He told them that, in his opinion, Rev. Henry B. Delany, who was then archdeacon of the colored convocation, was the best man for the office. Rev. M. A. Barber strongly represented the qualifications of the Rev. Mr. Baskerville, who had been recommended by Bishop Guerry, of South Carolina. Mr. Delany then withdrew from the conference, and Bishop Cheshire asked the colored clergy to express themselves frankly on their preference. Every one of them expressed the opinion that, while they thought Baskerville was an excellent man, they did not think he could compare with Delany in qualifications for the office of bishop. Of this unanimity of opinion, Bishop Cheshire remarked: "It was something of a surprise to me—for I really did not know how strong their feelings were."

When the convention proceeded to the election of a

suffragan bishop, Delany was the only man nominated. He received every vote of the clergy and laity. When he was presented to the convention and asked to say a few words, he simply remarked: "I cannot speak. I cannot utter what I feel. I thank you." Bishop Cheshire characterized his laconic expression as "about the best speech he could possibly have made." [3]

Archdeacon Delany was highly esteemed by both white and colored churchmen, and his election met with general satisfaction throughout the Diocese. Bishop Guerry wrote Bishop Cheshire that he thought Delany was "the logical man and I believe you have made a wise choice. . . . I envy you the privilege of having been the first Diocese in the Carolinas to take the lead in so far reaching a policy."

It will be remembered that while rector of St. Peter's, Bishop Cheshire had established in Charlotte a mission for Negroes, St. Michael and All Angels. Shortly after it was well started, Rev. Primus P. Alston, a colored priest, was placed in charge of the mission. Alston was an energetic and progressive man. He soon began a manual-training school for Negro boys and girls, which he called St. Michael's Industrial School. In time he erected buildings at a cost of about eight thousand dollars, raising almost all of the money by himself. After some twenty years of splendid work as head of this school, Rev. Mr. Alston died in 1910. Bishop Cheshire at once decided that something must be done to preserve the valuable work which Alston had carried on so successfully. Realizing the high regard which the people of Charlotte had for the man and his work, the Bishop determined to lay the question of the future of St. Michael's School before a body of representative citizens of Charlotte in the hope

Work Among the Colored People

of making it a civic enterprise, irrespective of denominational interests but still under the official administration of the diocesan bishop. Acting upon this decision, the Bishop called together in Charlotte a group of progressive men representing different denominations. He pointed out that the school was the property of the Diocese of North Carolina, that it had for more than twenty years done a great work for the community, and that no religious test was made an entrance requirement, although religious training was a part of the school's work. The Bishop then asked the group if it would act with him as a board of managers for the direction and maintenance of the school. The men displayed a sympathetic interest, and promised to co-operate with him in any plan for making permanent the work of the institution. The Bishop thereupon organized the Board of Managers of St. Michael's Industrial School, under whose control it continued to operate.

When Bishop Cheshire met his diocesan convention in 1912, he reported what he had done and asked for its endorsement of his action and its assent to the new plan for operating the school. The convention confirmed the Bishop's work and consented to his plan for continuing St. Michael's School. Thus, by his promptness and resourcefulness, he preserved for the church and the community of Charlotte a valuable institution.

Bishop Cheshire's work among the Negroes of his Diocese received recognition from the national church when, in 1911, he was elected chairman of the Advisory Council of the American Church Institute for Negroes. The Institute had been organized in 1906 for the purpose of aiding the larger Episcopal schools for Negroes, such as St. Augustine's, the Bishop Payne Divinity School, and others. From this time forward he received a number of invitations to speak in the dioceses of the North on various phases of the church's work among the Negroes of the South. One of his most interesting addresses on this subject was made before the Woman's Auxiliary of the Diocese of Long Island at its annual meeting in 1915.

In this address the Bishop declared that the fact the Negro was increasing in population meant to him that "God is not done with him. He has something for him to do." The Negro had not only survived his contact with a higher civilization, but had made in it a place for himself. "Protected and trained by his two and a half centuries of American slavery, the greatest blessing which up to this time he has ever known," the Negro had lived through emancipation and the "incalculable injustice of his premature enfranchisement." He was turning from false political and social aspirations and attempting to lay sound foundations for his moral and material development. Referring to the religion of the Negro, Bishop Cheshire observed that he found it very little different from that of the white man. He spoke of the Negro's gift of religious emotion, which might be dangerous, "yet it is a gift; and it is needed to give power and life to faith." The Bishop declared that the church set up a standard for the Negro to live by, it acknowledged him as a brother, and it gave him a definite place in its organization.

In answer to the question of what the Woman's Auxiliary could do for the Negro, Bishop Cheshire replied it should try to teach the colored churches to support themselves and to be willing and able to aid others. As for a particular work the organization could undertake, he emphasized the importance of hospital care. This was

Work Among the Colored People 107

a vital need and one which the Negro by himself could not supply.[4]

The address was well received, although a few of the ideas contained in it were doubtless a little disturbing to some of the listeners. The Bishop was fearless in expressing his convictions, and was ever ready to defend them when necessary.

St. Augustine's School for Negroes was founded in 1867 by North Carolina churchmen. It was built and maintained, however, by northern churchmen and agencies. While the school was not a diocesan institution, Bishop Cheshire throughout his episcopate gave it his full co-operation and support. He had a personal interest in the school, for his father had been one of the original incorporators. As ex-officio president of the Board of Trustees he kept in close contact with the development of St. Augustine's. Realizing that his state benefited most from the school, Bishop Cheshire time and time again urged his people to give it every encouragement and assistance within their means.

In appreciation of his services to St. Augustine's, the authorities of the school resolved to name a proposed new building for Bishop Cheshire. Of this decision, the presiding bishop, John Gardner Murray, remarked: "I can conceive of nothing more splendid that the Church or community could do than to erect at St. Augustine's a building in honor of Bishop Cheshire. The work itself is most deserving in every way, and the Bishop whose name you propose to have associated with it, is one of the greatest Bishops in our Church in his every relationship thereto." [5]

The dedication of the Cheshire Building at St. Augustine's College took place on Bishop Cheshire's eightieth birthday, March 27, 1930. In the course of the ceremony the Bishop delivered an address in which he traced the history of St. Augustine's from its establishment as a simple normal school to its present collegiate status. He touched upon the development of Negro education in the South since 1865, and emphasized the importance of this fact in the growth of a better relationship between the races. St. Augustine's, said the Bishop, in a larger sense represents the church's attitude towards the Negro problem in America and what it has done to solve that problem.

Dr. A. B. Hunter, principal of the school for twenty-five years, made a short talk in which he spoke of the Bishop's loyal support of St. Augustine's. He ascribed much of the institution's success to the "unfailing sympathy and material assistance of the Bishop." Towards the end of the ceremony a portrait of Bishop Cheshire, hanging in the hall of the new building, was unveiled.

Coming as it did towards the end of his life, this expression of appreciation from the colored people was a fitting close to the Bishop's work among the Negroes. He understood and respected his colored people, and in return they loved him and gave him their loyalty and confidence.

CHAPTER IX

Development and Conclusion of the Bishop's Work

In the first decade of his episcopate Bishop Cheshire laid the foundation for almost all of his future work. The remainder of his life was devoted to expansion and improvement. This program demanded all of his thought and energy and, as it progressed, became almost more than one man could administer. The Bishop never complained of being overworked, but when he realized he was no longer physically able to meet the demands of his office, he did not hesitate to ask for assistance.

A pleasant and interesting interlude in the routine of the Bishop's busy life was a trip to England in the summer of 1908. The object of the trip was to attend the Pan-Anglican Congress and the Lambeth Conference. The Bishop and Mrs. Cheshire sailed from New York and landed at Liverpool on May 28. Since the Pan-Anglican Congress was not to open for about two weeks, they spent the intervening time sightseeing and visiting friends. Among the many interesting places they visited was the old Abbey of Valle Crucis in Wales for which Bishop Ives had named his mission school in the mountains of North Carolina. The Bishop observed that here, however, there was no natural cruciform arrangement of valleys and streams which so distinguished his Valle Crucis mission.

The Pan-Anglican Congress was opened on June 15 by an impressive service held in Westminster Abbey. The Congress was composed of bishops, clergymen, laymen, and laywomen representing the Anglican communion from all parts of the world. There were six thousand delegates present, but they were divided into a number of sections for the discussion of every phase of church work. Bishop Cheshire attended the sessions of one of these sections every day, but he did not have time to enter in his journal much about the proceedings. On one occasion, when the topic for discussion was the church's work among the Negroes of North America, he was one of the speakers. He later remarked that he had scarcely warmed to his subject before his allotted time was gone.

On another occasion the Bishop was invited to a breakfast given by the Church Temperance Society. At the breakfast he was seated next to the Bishop of London, who was to preside over a meeting of the Society following the meal. In the course of conversation Bishop Cheshire remarked to the Bishop of London that "in America at least as far as concerned my part of it, drinking was unknown among women." The English prelate seemed to be greatly impressed by this statement. After the breakfast there were several scheduled speakers who talked on the problem of intemperance. They all agreed that the use of intoxicants in England as a whole had improved, but that the discouraging feature of the situation was the increased use of them by women. The Bishop of London announced that the meeeting would like to hear from the

Conclusion of the Bishop's Work

United States, and he would, therefore, call upon Bishop Cheshire for a few words. As he rose to speak, the Bishop of London said to him, "Tell them what you have been telling me." After commenting on the work of the Church Temperance Society, he complied with the request and added: "I believe it to be true of all parts of the United States that among the descendants of the original English, Scotch, and Scotch-Irish settlers of America, intemperance or the use of intoxicating drinks among the women is unknown, or so extremely rare as to amount to nothing in looking at the situation in its general aspect." [1] His audience displayed a keen interest in his views.

The Pan-Anglican Congress closed on June 24 with a service in St. Paul's Cathedral. Bishop Cheshire thought that the Congress was "the most remarkable religious gathering of recent times." He was particularly impressed by the deep interest the British public and press took in the proceedings of the Congress. The capacity of the great Albert Hall was taxed to hold the average daily attendance of twelve thousand persons.

The Lambeth Conference, which opened on July 5, did not attract as much attention as usual, since it followed so closely upon the Pan-Anglican Congress. Its work, however, was none the less significant in the life of the church. Bishop Cheshire considered its proceedings more interesting than those of 1897. He noted that the younger bishops took a more active part than they had in the previous Conference. He served as a member of the Committee on Foreign Missions.

Bishop Cheshire returned to England in the summer of 1920 to attend his third and final Lambeth Conference. He was then seventy years old but in good health and still capable of doing a full day's work. He regularly attended the sessions of the Conference, and manifested as much interest as ever in its work.

The Bishop was made a member of the Committee on Christianity and International Relations, which was to deal in particular with the League of Nations. He found the work of the committee very interesting, but later remarked that the American bishops on the committee found themselves in an embarrassing position, since the League of Nations had been made a political issue in the presidential campaign of that year.[2] Bishop Cheshire felt that this Lambeth Conference surpassed the two previous ones in the importance of the work accomplished and in the probable results. The Conference took much "wider and freer views" of the questions discussed. The Bishop observed that some of the speeches which were received with decided approval were strongly opposed to all that had been the traditional policy of the church.

Upon the close of the Conference Bishop and Mrs. Cheshire, accompanied by their friends, Dr. and Mrs. A. B. Hunter, spent a few weeks traveling on the Continent. The Bishop particularly enjoyed his visit to Switzerland, whose mountain scenery greatly impressed him. He always thought, however, that his North Carolina mountains were more beautiful and appealing than the more spectacular Alps. On one Sunday which the Cheshires and Hunters spent at Gletsch, Switzerland, the Bishop took his little party out into the country. In the presence of the great Rhône glacier with his "congregation" sitting on rocks about him, he read the Morning Prayer, omitting not one part of it.

In addition to his three visits to Europe, Bishop Cheshire made one other trip beyond the borders of the United

Conclusion of the Bishop's Work 113

States. In 1910 the Archbishop of the West Indies invited a number of American bishops to Jamaica to assist in the consecration of the churches which had been rebuilt on the island after the disastrous earthquake of 1907. Bishop Cheshire accepted the invitation and, as it turned out, was the sole representative of the American Episcopal Church. The consecration ceremonies took place in January, 1911. During his stay of about two weeks the Bishop participated in the consecration of five or six churches. Describing the ecclesiastical procession at one of the ceremonies, the *Daily News* of Kingston, Jamaica, commented: "There was then the stern Prelate of North Carolina just south of Mason and Dixon's line; Prelate of a vast domain many, many times the size of this island, and with a problem something like ours." This exaggerated description amused the Bishop a great deal. He enjoyed his visit, particularly riding about the island observing the customs and manners of the natives. He always took a keen pleasure in learning about new places and their people.

Turning now to diocesan affairs, we find Bishop Cheshire preparing to begin a long campaign to free St. Mary's School from its burdensome debt and to raise an adequate endowment for the institution. When he addressed the convention of 1912 he reminded the members that on October 15, 1913, he would complete twenty years as bishop of the Diocese of North Carolina. In his opinion, the most important work accomplished in this period was the establishment of St. Mary's as a diocesan school. The Bishop declared that he would like to celebrate his twentieth anniversary by paying off the debt on St. Mary's and by raising one hundred thousand dollars towards a permanent endowment. He wished, therefore, to devote much of his time for the next eighteen months to this end, and asked for the convention's support. The convention indorsed his suggestion and promised its co-operation.

At the convention of 1913 a special committee on an endowment for St. Mary's was appointed to work with the Bishop. Notwithstanding the efforts of Bishop Cheshire and the committee, very little money was raised by the anniversary of his consecration. Thus, the matter stood until 1916, when Bishop Cheshire proposed an exceedingly ambitious program. The plan called for raising fifty thousand dollars to retire the school's funded debt and to meet certain necessary expenses, one hundred thousand dollars as an endowment, and another hundred thousand for additions and improvements. It was further suggested that the dioceses of East Carolina, South Carolina, and the Jurisdiction of Asheville should be asked to co-operate in this endeavor. The convention adopted the plan, and the quota for Bishop Cheshire's Diocese was set at seventy-five thousand dollars.

The Bishop was untiring in his efforts to interest his people in the needs and promising future of St. Mary's. The program for raising the endowment was progressing well when the war disrupted its work, but the campaign was by no means abandoned. By the end of 1921 more than one hundred and forty-six thousand dollars had been pledged. Two years later the Bishop reported that St. Mary's School was free of all debt. The generous gifts to the school by Mr. Lawrence Holt and Mr. William A. Erwin, which followed shortly afterwards, gave the Bishop much pleasure and made him feel that the work which he considered the most important of his episcopate was now permanently established.

Conclusion of the Bishop's Work

When America entered the World War in 1917, Bishop Cheshire felt that President Wilson was fully justified in asking Congress for a declaration of war. Of the conflict he observed that, while America as a nation had committed errors and evils in the past, he believed that as far as the present war was concerned, "we know that we have no selfish purpose or desires." The Bishop was upholding a cause which was brought close home to him, for he had two sons who volunteered and later saw service in France. He had very definite ideas on duty to one's country, and little patience with those pacifists who held that a Christian could not go to war. In his opinion, such an argument was no more valid than it would be to say that one should not protect one's home and family against thieves and murderers. "We owe everything that we are—" declared the Bishop, "all that we have to our Country. We owe her ourselves." [3] In the course of the war he gave voice to these views in many of his sermons.

When the Bishop heard that a camp for training soldiers was to be established in Charlotte, he called together the Episcopal clergy of that city for a discussion of the problem of caring for the needs of thirty or forty thousand soldiers who were expected there. They devised plans for keeping open the parish houses of the several churches for the use of the soldiers, and the best means of caring for their religious life. The Bishop addressed a letter to the people of the Diocese asking them to give every possible assistance to their friends in Charlotte in this great responsibility.

As Bishop Cheshire was about to complete a quarter of a century as head of the Diocese of North Carolina, it was planned to celebrate the occasion with a special service in Calvary Church, Tarboro, on October 15, 1918. But when the time came for the celebration, it had to be postponed because of the influenza epidemic. It was finally held in Raleigh at the closing session of the convention of 1919. The Bishop delivered an address in which he traced the history of the Diocese during his episcopate. The convention then by a unanimous rising vote adopted the following resolution introduced by Dr. R. D. W. Connor:

> "That gratefully acknowledging our obligations to Almighty God for the many evidences of His Divine guidance in the affairs of His Church throughout this period of its history, we are especially grateful to Him for the love and care with which He has preserved the physical strength, the mental vigor and power, and the spiritual grace and consecration of our beloved Bishop. Resolved further, that this Diocese is greatly indebted to Bishop Cheshire for the sympathetic spirit, the unflagging zeal and never-failing wisdom and the statesmanlike vision with which, under God, he has directed its affairs, shaped its policies, and guided its growth and development; that we hope and pray he may long be spared to lead us in full strength and vigor of body, mind, and spirit; and that we take this opportunity of pledging to him our unswerving loyalty and undivided support in the prosecution of his labors for the spread of the Kingdom of God on earth." [4]

Dr. A. Burtis Hunter, for the clergy, and Governor Thomas Bickett, for the laity, brought to the Bishop messages of loyalty and affection. Mr. William A. Erwin presented the Bishop with a purse of gold from the people of the Diocese as a token of their love and esteem.

Conclusion of the Bishop's Work   117

Bishop Cheshire was deeply moved by these expressions from his clergy and laity. It would be difficult to find in any diocese a more sympathetic relationship between bishop and people.

As Bishop Cheshire advanced in years, changes were taking place in the church as in almost every other institution. Some of these he advocated, while others he accepted with regret. When the diocesan convention of 1919 met, a plan was introduced placing the administration of the affairs of the Diocese in the hands of the bishop and an executive council. Of the proposed plan Bishop Cheshire said that he thought it had "some advantages," but he earnestly hoped that the administration of the diocesan missions by the archdeacons would not in any way be changed. The archdeacons were a great assistance to the bishop in carrying on missionary work, and were invaluable in overseeing vacant parishes and missions. He referred to them as "the eyes of the Bishop in all matters of practical work," and stated that he wished to take this occasion to express his appreciation for the relief they had afforded him. In his opinion, whatever shortcomings could be ascribed to the present system of convocations under archdeacons were largely due to the lack of co-operation by the laity.

After considering several proposals, the convention adopted a plan of diocesan organization which provided for an executive committee to be elected by the convention. It was to be composed of the bishop as ex-officio chairman, three clergymen, three laymen, and three laywomen. The executive committee was to act as a co-ordinating and co-operating agent in diocesan work. The convention also provided the bishop with a secretary who should likewise serve as secretary of the executive committee. The functions of the archdeacons were not at this time altered. Several years later, however, the personnel of the executive committee and the scope of its influence were enlarged. Also, a field secretary, who was to oversee missionary work, was employed. These innovations made the old system of convocations and archdeacons unnecessary, and it was accordingly abolished.

The Bishop observed with regret the abolition of the office of archdeacon but acquiesced in it, since the majority of the clergy and laity preferred the new system of administration. In his annual address of 1929 he paid a final tribute to his archdeacons. He asserted that the missionary work had never been so well looked after as under their supervision, and that he would not have been able to advance this phase of his work without their invaluable assistance.

When Bishop Cheshire was entering upon his seventieth year, he felt little impairment of his physical strength and had no desire to diminish his episcopal duties. He realized, however, that others might feel he was growing too old to carry on the work alone. Placing the affairs of the church above any personal considerations, he asked the convention of 1919 whether he should continue to administer the Diocese without assistance or adopt some other course. The Bishop then retired, and the convention sitting as a committee of the whole considered its reply. Dr. Richard H. Lewis introduced a resolution which was unanimously adopted. It declared that the affairs of the Diocese had in no way been neglected; that there was no evidence of failure of the Bishop's physical or mental faculties; and that the convention was confident that he would ask for assistance when he felt it was necessary. The confidence his people placed

Conclusion of the Bishop's Work 119

in him, as expressed in this resolution, gave Bishop Cheshire much pleasure and encouragement.

In the spring of 1922 the Bishop informed the Standing Committee of the Diocese that he had been urged by several physicians and laymen to curtail his work and to request the convention for assistance. The Standing Committee promptly advised him to propose the election of a bishop coadjutor. Accordingly, on April 21, he addressed a letter to the clergy in which he announced his intention to ask the approaching diocesan convention to consider the question of electing a bishop coadjutor. The Bishop felt the clergy and laity should be informed of his purpose in order that they might give this important subject thoughtful consideration before the meeting of the convention.

On May 16, at the Church of the Good Shepherd, Raleigh, the convention met and immediately took up the question of giving the Bishop assistance in his work. After consideration it resolved that a bishop coadjutor should be elected. Bishop Cheshire then gave his consent to the election, and assigned to whoever should hold the new office the episcopal oversight of the Convocation of Charlotte and the personal supervision of all postulants and candidates for Holy Orders of the Diocese.

The nominations for bishop coadjutor took place on the evening of the second day. After six ballots were taken, the Rev. Edwin Anderson Penick, Rector of St. Peter's Church, Charlotte, was elected. He received thirty-two clerical votes and twenty-four from the laity. The choice of the convention met with general satisfaction throughout the Diocese. Concerning the election, Bishop Cheshire declared: "We believe that the Spirit of God effectuates with His presence, His guidance, His blessing, the solemn functions of the Body of Christ. And never, I make bold to say, did we feel more sure of the Divine presence, guidance and blessing, than in the solemn hour of the choosing of our Bishop Coadjutor. Among the many happy and helpful experiences of my Episcopate, and of my life, I remember that as one of the best." [5]

On October 15, 1922, the twenty-ninth anniversary of Bishop Cheshire's consecration, Rev. Edwin A. Penick, D.D., was consecrated bishop coadjutor in St. Peter's Church, Charlotte. He entered upon the duties of his office almost immediately thereafter. From that time until the death of Bishop Cheshire the two men worked together in perfect harmony. Although they did not always agree on diocesan policy, they never allowed a difference of opinion to mar their affectionate relationship.

Bishop Cheshire gradually placed more responsibility on Bishop Penick as he became better acquainted with the work of the Diocese. A characteristic act of Bishop Cheshire's, and one which claimed the admiration of his people, was the turning over of the work at Chapel Hill to Bishop Penick's supervision. The Chapel of the Cross at Chapel Hill had been the Bishop's first parish and he had always retained for it a deep affection. Therefore, it was a personal sacrifice for him to relinquish it to another. He felt that, due to the peculiar nature of the work at Chapel Hill, it should be under the guidance of a younger man.

As Bishop Cheshire grew older he began to plan how best he could provide for his wife and daughter when they would no longer be able to live at Ravenscroft, the Bishop's house. He decided to build a small apart-

Conclusion of the Bishop's Work

ment house in Raleigh, which would produce an income as well as provide a home for them. When the house was completed he advertised the apartments for rent only to families with children. He thought the frequent practice of denying apartments to persons with children was most unfair and, therefore, determined to make his house an exception. This was typical of the Bishop, who loved children and large families.

In building his apartment house Bishop Cheshire had to borrow a part of the cost of its construction. Speaking of this to Bishop Penick, he remarked he hoped to live four years longer since by that time his loan would be retired. Recalling this observation Bishop Penick decided to raise a sum of money from among the people of the Diocese to relieve the Bishop of this care. The money was raised by the time the diocesan convention met in the spring of 1924 at Winston-Salem. It was a fitting time and place for the presentation of the gift, since it was at Winston-Salem thirty years before that Bishop Cheshire presided over his first convention. The gift, which amounted to $4,273, was presented to the Bishop from the people of the Diocese by Dr. Richard H. Lewis, who said in part: "My dear Bishop: By your strong and vigorous intellect, your wide and accurate learning, your public spirit, your unspotted character, and a personality of unaffected friendship, you have come to be—in the words of another—'one of the best known and best loved men in our State.'" Referring to this generous expression of affection, Bishop Cheshire remarked that he could never "cease to feel grateful to him whose generosity conceived the idea, and to the many kind friends who responded to his suggestion, and transmuted his thoughts into act."

At this convention the Bishop delivered an address in which he briefly reviewed the high points in the thirty years of his episcopate. He declared he wished to repeat a major point he had made in his first episcopal address in 1894, namely, the importance of realizing the "common bond of union in the Diocese by becoming interested in common Diocesan work." During the past three decades Bishop Cheshire had accomplished more than any of his predecessors in breaking down parochialism by arousing in his people a lively interest in diocesan enterprises. The Bishop concluded the review of his work by saying that the past thirty years had been happy ones, "years in which I have received much love, consideration, and kindness from all our people, clerical and lay."

The unusual and praiseworthy feature of the general esteem in which Bishop Cheshire was held in North Carolina was the demonstration of that esteem during his lifetime. The churchmen did not wait until his death to eulogize him and to erect memorials in his honor. On many occasions and in many different ways he was made to realize the high place which he held in the hearts of his people.

After completing thirty-five years as bishop of the Diocese of North Carolina, a longer period than any of his predecessors, Bishop Cheshire felt that he must give up the greater part of his work. He therefore informed the convention of 1929 that he was turning over to Bishop Penick the general administration of the entire Diocese. He thought that the ever-increasing and more complicated work of the church required a younger and more vigorous man, one, as he expressed it, "more adaptable and more in sympathy with changing conditions and methods." Of Bishop Penick he said: "We have one whom we all believe to be eminently fitted to carry on the Diocese with success and with the confidence, sympathy and affection of all." Bishop Cheshire did not intend, however, to relinquish all of his duties. He retained for himself the episcopal oversight of about one-third of the parishes and missions, the keeping of the diocesan register, and the requisite business before the Standing Committee. The parishes which he reserved for his own visitations were all located within a convenient distance from Raleigh.

Bishop Cheshire was not present at the convention of 1929 because of the serious illness of Mrs. Cheshire. Bishop Penick read his address. It was the first diocesan convention that he had failed to attend since 1876 when he had been present as a lay delegate. Mrs. Cheshire died before the convention adjourned. Accordingly, resolutions of sympathy for the Bishop were adopted, and a committee was appointed to represent the convention at Mrs. Cheshire's funeral. The death of his wife was a great loss to the Bishop; their life of thirty years together had been happy and congenial. Mrs. Cheshire had been a generous mother to his small children, and a helpful and devoted wife.

Although his strength was gradually failing, Bishop Cheshire displayed during the next three years a remarkable activity. For one of his years he preserved an unusually tolerant attitude towards the many religious, social, and political changes of the day. When, on his eightieth birthday, he was asked what he thought of the youth of today, the Bishop replied: "The world is a much better place than it was when I was a young man. ... Young people today have more personal religion than they did then." [6] While he disapproved of much that was done by the youth of today, he thought that his parents must have had much of the same sort of disapproval of his own generation. "When people talk," said the Bishop, "of the degeneration of the morals and manners of the present, and praise the good old times and old time religion, as being so much superior to the present, they do not know what the old times were, and in my opinion, they are often speaking nonsense. That is my very serious opinion."[7] In making this observation he did not mean to depreciate the religion of his forefathers, for no one had a greater respect and veneration for the past.

During the last year of his life Bishop Cheshire filled almost all of his regular visitations in the eastern part of the Diocese. In addition, he spent ten days, in the month of July, visiting the country churches in the counties of Rowan, Mecklenburg, Davie, and Iredell. In the course of these visitations he called on forty families in the several parishes and missions. Such activity in midsummer would have taxed the strength of a far younger man, but it did not appear to trouble the Bishop. At the time, he wrote his son that although the heat was very severe, he noticed it no more than if he had been doing nothing. In June of 1932 the Bishop went to Hartford, Connecticut, to assist in the consecration of a new chapel at his alma mater, Trinity College. He enjoyed the trip thoroughly, renewing some of his old friendships and making new ones.

By the fall of 1932 Bishop Cheshire's health was greatly impaired, but he continued his visitations through December 11. On that day he performed his last service. He confirmed a class of fifteen persons in the Church of the Good Shepherd, Raleigh, but was not able to preach the sermon. A few days later he went to Charlotte for treatment by a specialist. Shortly after entering the hospital, however, he became gradually worse. On December 27,

Conclusion of the Bishop's Work 125

at six-thirty in the evening, the Diocese of North Carolina lost its beloved Bishop.

It was unusually difficult for the people of the Diocese to realize that Bishop Cheshire would no longer be with them. He had possessed such a lovable and dynamic personality, had so largely molded the character of the Diocese, and had been its Bishop for so long that his people found it hard to associate the idea of death with him. He had baptized, confirmed, or married many of them, had entered sympathetically into the pleasures and problems of their secular as well as their spiritual lives, and thus endeared himself to them to an extent far beyond the capacity of most men. In the words of the Presiding Bishop, James DeWolf Perry: "It is impossible to foresee a time when his influence will not be felt, his penetrating mind will not be esteemed or when his name will cease to be held in grateful and loving remembrance."

THE CHAPEL OF THE CROSS, CHAPEL HILL
From a drawing by Mary de B. Graves

Notes

CHAPTER I. YOUTH AND MANHOOD

1. Joseph Blount Cheshire, "Some Account of My Life for My Children," *Carolina Churchman*, March, 1934. Hereafter, this work is cited simply as "Some Account of My Life."
2. This manuscript was written on February 12, 1866. It is owned by Mr. J. B. Cheshire, Jr., of Raleigh.
3. Cheshire, "Some Account of My Life," *Carolina Churchman*, May, 1934.
4. *Ibid.*, December, 1934.
5. *Ibid.*
6. *Ibid.*, February, 1935.
7. *Ibid.*

CHAPTER II. DEACON AND PRIEST

1. Cheshire, "Some Account of My Life," *Carolina Churchman*, May, 1935.
2. *Ibid.*, April, 1935.
3. *Church Messenger*, August 4, 1881.
4. Joseph B. Cheshire, "Autobiography," pp. 229-230, a manuscript work owned by Mr. J. B. Cheshire, Jr.
5. *Ibid.*, p. 230.
6. *Ibid.*, pp. 231-232.
7. *Ibid.*, p. 256.

CHAPTER III. SAINT PETER'S PARISH

1. Cheshire to his wife, November 23, 1905, Cheshire Manuscripts, owned by Mr. J. B. Cheshire, Jr., Raleigh.
2. Cheshire, "Autobiography," p. 315.
3. *Ibid.*, p. 322.
4. *Ibid.*, p. 345.
5. Cheshire to Bishop Lyman, April 6, 1886, Joseph Blount Cheshire Papers, University of North Carolina Library.

6. Bishop Lyman to Cheshire, October 17, 1888, Joseph Blount Cheshire Papers, University of North Carolina Library.
7. A. W. Dodge to Cheshire, July 6, 1891, Bishop Joseph Blount Cheshire Papers, North Carolina Historical Commission.
8. Cheshire, "Autobiography," p. 382.

CHAPTER IV. ELECTION TO THE EPISCOPATE

1. Cheshire to Nannie C. Hoke, February 16, 1891, Bishop Joseph Blount Cheshire Papers, North Carolina Historical Commission.
2. Rev. Robert B. Owens to L. F. London, July 8, 1938. Mr. Owens was a member of the adjourned convention of 1893. This letter contains a description of the proceedings of that convention.
3. Cheshire to Dr. Joseph B. Cheshire, Sr., June 29, 1893, Bishop Joseph Blount Cheshire Papers, North Carolina Historical Commission.
4. Cheshire to Sallie Badger Hoke, July 3, 1893, Bishop Joseph Blount Cheshire Papers, North Carolina Historical Commission.
5. Rev. Francis J. Murdoch in an open letter to Rev. E. A. Osborne, 1893, Bishop Joseph Blount Cheshire Papers, North Carolina Historical Commission.

CHAPTER V. FIRST YEARS IN THE EPISCOPACY

1. *Journal of the Convention of the Diocese of North Carolina* (1894), p. 64.
2. Joseph B. Cheshire, *Milnor Jones, Deacon and Missionary*, p. 28.
3. *Ibid.*, p. 53.
4. *Journal of the Convention of the Missionary Jurisdiction of Asheville* (1896), p. 51.
5. *Ibid.*, pp. 50-51.
6. Cheshire to his wife, October 2, 1901, Cheshire Manuscripts, owned by Mr. J. B. Cheshire, Jr., Raleigh.
7. Joseph B. Cheshire, *Fifty Years of Church Life in North Carolina*, p. 6.
8. Joseph B. Cheshire, Journal of 1897, p. 96, a manuscript account of his visit to England and the Continent in the summer of 1897, owned by Mr. J. B. Cheshire, Jr., Raleigh.
9. Nicholas Collin Hughes, "Some Memories of Bishop Cheshire." This manuscript was written for L. F. London and is in his possession.
10. *Journal of the Convention of the Diocese of North Carolina* (1896), pp. 61-62.
11. Cheshire to his wife, November 7, 1899, Cheshire Manuscripts, owned by Mr. J. B. Cheshire, Jr., Raleigh.
12. The Raleigh *News and Observer*, October 15, 1903.

Notes

CHAPTER VI. MAN AND BISHOP

1. *Carolina Churchman*, April, 1931.

CHAPTER VII. HISTORIAN

1. Cheshire, "Some Account of My Life," *Carolina Churchman*, January, 1935.
2. Walter Clark to Cheshire, May 24, 1893, Bishop Joseph Blount Cheshire Papers, North Carolina Historical Commission.
3. Cheshire, "Autobiography," p. 360.
4. *Ibid.*, pp. 414-418.
5. The Raleigh *News and Observer*, December 4, 1931.

CHAPTER VIII. WORK AMONG THE COLORED PEOPLE

1. Cheshire to his wife, August 25, 1905, Cheshire Manuscripts, owned by Mr. J. B. Cheshire, Jr., Raleigh.
2. *Journal of the Convention of the Diocese of North Carolina* (1907), p. 72.
3. Bishop Cheshire to Bishop Guerry, May 17, 1918, Joseph Blount Cheshire Papers, University of North Carolina Library.
4. Joseph B. Cheshire, Manuscript Address, Cheshire Manuscripts, owned by Mr. J. B. Cheshire, Jr., Raleigh.
5. *Carolina Churchman*, May, 1929.

CHAPTER IX. DEVELOPMENT AND CONCLUSION OF THE BISHOP'S WORK

1. Joseph B. Cheshire, "Our Summer, 1908," a journal of his visit to England for the Pan-Anglican Congress and the Lambeth Conference, owned by Mr. J. B. Cheshire, Jr., Raleigh.
2. Joseph B. Cheshire, "England, 1920," a journal of his trip to England for the Lambeth Conference and of his visit to France and Switzerland, owned by Mr. J. B. Cheshire, Jr., Raleigh.
3. Sermon on Patriotism and the War, Joseph Blount Cheshire Papers, University of North Carolina Library.
4. *Journal of the Convention of the Diocese of North Carolina* (1919), p. 51.
5. *Ibid.* (1923), p. 84.
6. The Raleigh *News and Observer*, March 28, 1930.
7. *Carolina Churchman*, April, 1930.

Published Writings of Joseph Blount Cheshire

Address of the Right Rev. Joseph Blount Cheshire, Bishop of North Carolina, on the Occasion of the Dedication of the Memorial Vestibule in Christ Church, Raleigh, to the Glory of God and in the Memory of Richard Henry Lewis, December 18, 1927. Charlottesville, Va., n.d.

"Baptism of Virginia Dare," anniversary address, delivered on Roanoke Island by Rt. Rev. Joseph Blount Cheshire, D.D., August 18, 1910, *North Carolina Booklet*, Vol. X, no. 4.

Bishop Atkinson and the Church in the Confederacy. Raleigh, 1909.

"The Bishops of North Carolina—When the State Was One Diocese," *The Carolina Churchman*, November, 1910–February, 1911.

The Church in the Confederate States: A History of the Protestant Episcopal Church in the Confederate States. New York: Longmans, Green and Co., 1912.

"The Church in the Province of North Carolina," in *Sketches of Church History in North Carolina*, edited by Bishop Cheshire.

"Decay and Revival, 1800–1830," in *Sketches of Church History in North Carolina*, edited by Bishop Cheshire.

"Dr. Richard H. Lewis; An Intimate Sketch by a Life-long Friend," *The Carolina Churchman*, October, 1926.

The Early Conventions: held at Tarborough Anno Domini 1790, 1793 and 1794. The first effort to organize the Church in North Carolina. Collected from original sources and now first published. With introduction and brief notes, Raleigh, 1882.

"The Early Rectors of Christ Church," *Centennial Ceremonies held in Christ Church Parish, Raleigh, North Carolina, A.D. 1921. Including Historical Addresses.* Raleigh, 1922.

"Entries in an Old Bible which was Formerly in the Possession of Miss Chloe Coward," *North Carolina Historical and Genealogical Register*, July, 1903.

Fifty Years of Church Life in North Carolina, an Address by the Rt. Rev. Joseph Blount Cheshire, D.D., Bishop of North Carolina, on the Fiftieth Anniversary of the Rev. Robert B. Drane, D.D., as Rector of St. Paul's Church, Edenton, N. C. All Saints' Day, 1926. Edenton, n.d.

"First Settlers in North Carolina Not Religious Refugees: A Study in Origins," *North Carolina Booklet*, Vol. V, no. 4.

Fragments of Colonial Church History: 1. Public Libraries. n.p., 1886.

"The Fundamental Constitutions of Carolina, and Religious Liberty in the Province of North Carolina," *Historical Magazine of the Protestant Episcopal Church*, Vol. I, no. 4.

An Historical Address Delivered in Saint Matthew's Church, Hillsboro, N. C., on Sunday, August 24, 1924. Being the One Hundredth Anniversary of the Parish. Durham, 1925.

"An Historical Sketch of the Church in Edgecombe County, North Carolina," *Church Messenger*, August 17–September 21, 1880.

"How Our Church Came to North Carolina," *The Spirit of Missions*, May, 1918.

Milnor Jones, Deacon and Missionary. Raleigh, 1920.

Nonnulla: Memories, Stories, and Traditions, More or Less Authentic, About North Carolina. Chapel Hill: The University of North Carolina Press, 1930.

"The Office of Solicitor General of North Carolina," *University of North Carolina Magazine*, May, 1894.

"The Personnel of the North Carolina Convention of 1788," *Publications of the Southern History Association*, Vol. III, 1899.

Published Writings

A Priest to the Temple or, The Country Parson, His Character and Rule of Holy Life, by George Herbert, with an Introduction and brief notes by the Bishop of North Carolina. New York: Thomas Whittaker, Inc., 1908.

Public Worship in the Church. A Charge to the Clergy of the Diocese of North Carolina delivered at the meeting of the Convocations of Raleigh and Charlotte, in October, 1912. Also a Pastoral Letter to the Clergy and Laity of the Diocese. n.p., n.d.

Saint Peter's Church, Charlotte, North Carolina—Thirty Years of its Life and Work, 1863-1893. Charlotte, 1921.

"A Sermon; Preached in St. John's Church, Fayetteville, the Sunday next before Advent, November 24, 1889, at the Centennial of the Fayetteville Convention of 1789," *University of North Carolina Magazine*, Vol. XI, no. 4.

Sketches of Church History in North Carolina, Addresses and Papers by the Clergymen and Laymen of the Dioceses of North and East Carolina. Wilmington, 1892.

"Some Account of My Life for My Children," *Carolina Churchman*, January, 1934–May, 1935.

"White Haven Church and the Rev. Robert Johnston Miller," in *Sketches of Church History in North Carolina*, edited by Bishop Cheshire.

"Why Judge Haywood Left North Carolina," *University of North Carolina Magazine*, January, 1895.

"Wilmington, the Free Town of the Cape Fear," in *Historic Towns of the Southern States*, by Lyman P. Powell. New York: The Knickerbocker Press, 1900.

Index

A

Abbey of Valle Crucis, 109
Adams, Rev. Samuel F., 59
"A. H. W.," poem, 17
Albemarle section, 2, 89
Alpha Delta Phi, 11
Alston, Rev. Primus P., 31, 76, 104
Alumnae Association of St. Mary's School, 64
American Church Institute for Negroes, Cheshire elected to, 105
"Annals of the Church in the Province of North Carolina," MS by Cheshire, 91
Archdeacons, Cheshire's estimate of, 117-118
Ashe County, 57-58
Atkinson, Bishop Thomas, 18-19, 21; on division of Diocese, 35; sketch of by Cheshire, 94-95

B

Bakersville, N. C., 58
Baltimore, 13; practices law in, 14-15
Barber, Rev. M. A., 103
Barrett, Rev. Robert S., 47, 48
Barrows, Rev. W. S., 49
Baskerville, Rev. Erasmus L., 103

Battle, President Kemp P., 19, 22, 39
Battle, Richard H., 75
Beach Cliff Schoolhouse, 34
Beaver Creek, 58-59
Bickett, Gov. Thomas, 116
Bishop of Georgia, Cheshire considered for, 41
Bishop Payne Divinity School, 105
Bixby, Robert F., 10
Blount, Elizabeth, 2
Blount, Joseph, 2
Bridgers, Cheshire, and Bridgers, firm of, 15
Bridgers, Col. John L., 15
Bridgers, John L., Jr., 15
Bronson, Rev. Benjamin S., institutional work in Charlotte, 28-29
Burlington, N. C., Cheshire is called to church at, 25
Buxton, Rev. Jarvis, 40, 91

C

Calvary Church, Tarboro, 2, 3, 35; Cheshire receives call to, 41; Cheshire consecrated in, 52-53
Canterbury, Archbishop of, 67
Capers, Bishop Ellison, 53, 66
Chapel Hill, 19-20; Cheshire gives work in to Bishop Penick, 120

Chapel of the Cross, Cheshire becomes rector of, 19-20
Charlotte, Cheshire begins work in, 27
Cheshire, Annie, 44
Cheshire, Annie Gray, Bishop's sister, 4
Cheshire, Annie Webb (Mrs. Joseph Blount), 17, 22, 44; death of, 67
Cheshire, Elizabeth Mitchell (Mrs. Joseph Blount), 69; death of, 123
Cheshire, Elizabeth Toole, 23, 44
Cheshire, Godfrey, 44
Cheshire, James Webb, 44
Cheshire, John, the Bishop's grandfather, 2
Cheshire, Dr. Joseph Blount, Sr., 2, 3, 4, 7, 10
Cheshire, Bishop Joseph Blount, birth, 4; early education, 4-6; practices law, 14-17; marries Annie Webb, 17; ordained deacon, 19; rector, Chapel of the Cross, 19-26; ordained priest, 25; rector, St. Peter's, Charlotte, 27 ff.; Negro work in Charlotte, 30-31; in diocesan conventions, 34-39; views on episcopate, 47; elected assistant bishop, 50; on Missionary Jurisdiction of Asheville, 60-63; St. Mary's School, 63-66; death of Annie Webb Cheshire, 67; marries Elizabeth Mitchell, 69; in the General Convention, 69-70; on public worship, 71-72; on fishing and hunting, 77-79; on divorce question, 81-84; on national prohibition, 84-85; as a father, 86-87; on racial episcopate, 101-104; asks for assistance, 119; death of Elizabeth Mitchell Cheshire, 123; on youth of today, 123-124; death of, 125

Cheshire, Joseph Blount, Jr., 44, 77
Cheshire, Katherine Drane, 4
Cheshire, Sarah, 44, 79
Cheshire, Theophilus Parker, 4
Cheshire Building, St. Augustine's, 107
Christ Church, Raleigh, 48
Church in the Confederate States, discussion of, 94-96
Churchman, The, 95
Church Messenger, 23, 25, 90
Church of the Good Shepherd, Raleigh, 75, 119; Cheshire's last service, 124
Church Temperance Society, of England, 110-111
Church Times, 95
Clark, Gov. Henry, 88
Clark, Judge Walter, 89
Colonial Records of North Carolina, 89, 91
Connor, R. D. W., resolution on the Bishop, 116
Convocation for Colored Work, 74
Convocation of Charlotte, 74, 119
Convocation of Raleigh, 74
Curtis, Dr. M. Ashley, 3, 53

D

Davidson College, 33
Deerfield, Mass., 10
Delany, Rev. Henry B., 76; elected suffragan bishop, 103-104
Devereaux, Thomas P., 2
Division of the Diocese, 35-36
Dodge, Rev. A. W., 42
Drane, Dr. Robert B., on Cheshire's sermons, 80-81
Dudley, Bishop T. U., 53
Durham, N. C., 20; Cheshire organizes church in, 23-25

Index 137

E

Edenton, N. C., home of Cheshire's ancestors, 2
Edenton Academy, 2
Edgecombe County, 19-20; history of church in, 88-89
Eliot, George, quotation from, 100
Ellicott City, 1, 12
Episcopal School for Boys, Raleigh, 2
Erwin, William A., 114, 116
Executive council, formed, 117-118

F

France, Cheshire visits, 68
Fundamental Constitutions, Cheshire discusses, 97

G

General Convention, Cheshire elected deputy to, 40; on racial episcopate, 102
George, Rev. T. M. N., nominated assistant bishop, 48
Glenn, Gov. Robert B., 83
Gletsch, Switzerland, 112
Good Samaritan Hospital, 42-43, 99
Graves, Professor Ralph, 22
Graves' school, Granville County, 7
Guerry, Bishop William A., 103, 104
Guild of St. Martin, 32

H

Halifax, 3
Harding, Rev. Nathaniel H., nominated assistant bishop, 48
Hartford, Conn., 8, 10

Herbert, George, 93, 94
Hillsboro, N. C., 20; Cheshire studies law in, 13-14
Historiographer, Cheshire elected, 90
Holler, Bill, 77-78
Holmes, Rev. Lucian, 29
Holt, Lawrence, 114
Honesty, Cheshire writes essay on, 7
Honorary degrees, given Cheshire, 93
Hooper, George G., Cheshire's law partner, 14-15
Hooper, Professor J. de Berniere, 22
Hooper and Cheshire, firm of, 15
Horner, Bishop Junius Moore, consecrated bishop, 63
Howard, Judge George, 14
Howard and Perry, firm of, 14
Hunter, Dr. A. B., 108, 112, 116

I

Iredell County, 42
Ireland, Cheshire visits, 68
Ives, Bishop Levi Silliman, 2, 3; work at Valle Crucis, 56, 59; sketch of by Cheshire, 94

J

Jackson, Bishop Henry M., 47
Jamaica, Cheshire visits, 113
Johns, Bishop John, advice to young clergymen, 21
Johnston, William H., 5
Joint convention of 1890, 91-92
Jones, Hamilton C., 28
Jones, Rev. Milnor, mission work in the mountains, 56-59; Cheshire's estimate of, 60; life of by Cheshire, 96
Jones, Sam, 43-44
Jurisdiction of Asheville, formation of, 61-63

Index

K

Kerfoot, President of Trinity College, 9

L

Lambeth Conference, Cheshire attends, 67-68, 109, 111-112
Lenten services, Cheshire on, 73
Lewis, Nell Battle, tribute to the Bishop, 86
Lewis, Dr. Richard H., 5, 7, 13, 118; Cheshire's best man, 17; tribute to Cheshire, 121
Lloyd, Rev. Arthur S., nominated assistant bishop, 49
Long Creek Township, 33-34
Louisburg, N. C., 5
Louisburg Academy, Cheshire attends, 6
Lucas, Rev. Henry, 41
Lyman, Bishop Theodore Benedict, 21, 24, 25, 34, 53; on division of Diocese, 35; estimate of Cheshire's work in Charlotte, 41; asks for assistance, 46, 48; death of, 54; sketch of by Cheshire, 94

M

McCoy, Columbus W., 33
Mallett, Dr. William P., 22
Marshall, Dr. Matthias M., 19, 35; nominated assistant bishop, 48
Maryland, 9, 12
Mecklenburg County, missions in, 42
Meredith, Rev. Reuben, 79
Methodist Church Conference, 83
Missionary bishops for Negro work, 101-102
Mitchell, Elizabeth Lansdale, marries Bishop Cheshire, 69; death of, 123
Mitchell, Rev. Walter A., 69
Mitchell County, 57-58
Monreath, summer home of the Bishop's father, 5, 12
Monroe, N. C., Cheshire organizes church in, 32
Mooresville, N. C., 33
Murdoch, Dr. Francis J., Cheshire's estimate of, 47; nominated assistant bishop, 48; nominates Cheshire, 48; on Cheshire's election as bishop, 51
Murray, Bishop John Gardner, estimate of Cheshire, 107
Music in the church, Cheshire on, 73

N

Negro, religion of the, 106
Newsome, A. R., estimate of Cheshire as an historian, 98
Niles, Professor William W., 9
Nonnulla, vii, 79; discussion of, 97

O

Orkneys, Cheshire visits, 68
Osborne, Rev. Edwin A., takes work at Monroe and Long Creek, 32, 34; founds Thompson Orphanage, 42
Outlook, 95

P

Palmer, Professor George H., 94
Pamlico Banking and Insurance Company, 15, 19
Pan-Anglican Congress, 109-111
Parker, Elizabeth Toole, 4
Parker, Mary Toole, 4
Parker, Theophilus, 4
Pastoral Letter, by Cheshire, 72-73

Index 139

Penick, Bishop Edwin A., elected bishop coadjutor, 119; proposes gift for Cheshire, 121, 122
Perry, Bishop James DeWolf, tribute to Cheshire, 125
Phi Kappa, Cheshire's fraternity, 11
Pittsboro, N. C., 19
Polk County, 57
Portrait of the Bishop, 108
Presbyterian Synod, 83
Pynchon, Professor at Trinity, 10

Q

Quaker settlements in North Carolina, 89
Quin, Rev. Charles C., 30-32
Quintard, Bishop Charles T., 53

R

Racial episcopate, 103
Ravenscroft, Bishop John Stark, 47; sketch of by Cheshire, 94
Ravenscroft, Raleigh, home of the Bishop, 120
Roanoke River swamp, Bishop hunts in, 78
Rockingham, N. C., 33
Ruffin, Chief Justice Thomas, 13
Ruffin, William K., Cheshire studies law under, 13-14, 16

S

St. Ambrose Church, Raleigh, 76
St. Augustine's School, 105, 107-108
St. Clement's Hall, Cheshire teaches at, 1, 12-13, 16
St. Luke's Church, Tarboro, Cheshire holds first service as bishop in, 53

St. Mark's Church, Mecklenburg County, 25; organized, 34
St. Martin's Church, Charlotte, organized, 31
St. Mary's School, founded, 63-64; Cheshire's opinion of, 64; established as a church school, 64-66; Cheshire's daughters attend, 87; debt on, 113-114; endowment for, 114
St. Matthew's Church, Hillsboro, Cheshire married in, 17; Cheshire is called to, 25
St. Michael and All Angels, Charlotte, organized, 30, 31, 99
St. Michael's Industrial School, Charlotte, 104-105
St. Paul's Church, Edenton, 2, 80
St. Paul's Church, Macon, Ga., Cheshire receives call to, 41
St. Paul's Church, Winston-Salem, 25, 55
St. Peter's Church, Charlotte, 28, 36; Cheshire is called to, 26
St. Peter's Home and Hospital, organized, 29, 30
St. Philip's Church, Durham, 24-25
Saluda conference, 66
Saunders, Col. William L., 89-90
Scotland, Cheshire visits, 68
Scotland Neck, 3
Sermons, Cheshire discusses, 21-22
Sessums, Bishop Davis, 53
Shepherd, John Avery, 12
Smedes, Dr. Aldert, 63
Smedes, Dr. Bennett, 63, 64, 66
Smedes, Rev. John E. C., 19, 25; verses to Cheshire, 51-52
Society of the Cincinnati, Cheshire becomes member of, 93
State Literary and Historical Association, Cheshire elected president of, 97
Strange, Rev. Robert B., 92
Suffragan bishops, for Negro work, 101-104

Index

Sutton, Rev. Robert B., 19, 20
Switzerland, Cheshire visits, 68, 112

T

Tarboro, N. C., 14-15, 17; description of, 2
Tarboro Building and Loan Association, 15-16
Tarboro Male Academy, Cheshire attends, 5, 7, 13
Thompson Orphanage, Charlotte, 42
Trinity Church, Scotland Neck, 3
Trinity College, Hartford, Conn., Cheshire enters, 8-9; graduates from, 11-12; confers degree on Cheshire, 93; Cheshire visits, 124
Tryon, N. C., 56
"Tuttle Prize," Cheshire wins, 11

U

University of North Carolina, 5, 6, 8, 19, 87; confers degree on Cheshire, 93
University of the South, Cheshire made trustee of, 39-40; Cheshire's son attends, 87; confers degree on Cheshire, 93

V

Valle Crucis, Cheshire revives work at, 56-57, 59

W

Watauga County, missions in, 57-58
Watauga River, 56, 77
Watson, Bishop Alfred A., 25, 53
Webb, Annie Huske, Cheshire meets, 16; marries Cheshire, 17; death of, 67
Weed, Bishop Edwin G., 53
Weeks, Stephen B., 49 n.
West Indies, Archbishop of, 113
Wetmore, Rev. George B., 34
Whipple, Bishop Henry B., 47
Wilkes, John, 27-28, 32
Wilkes, Mrs. John, 42-43
Wilkinson, Frank S., 5, 7-8
Williams, Bishop John, 10-11
Wilson, President Woodrow, 115
Winchester, Rev. J. R., 47
Windsor, N. C., 3
Winston, Professor George T., 22

Y

York, Archbishop of, Cheshire visits, 68

www.ingramcontent.com/pod-product-compliance
Lightning Source LLC
Chambersburg PA
CBHW030114010526
44116CB00005B/249